AN ADULT*ACTIVITY BOOK.

✕ BEYOND ✕

BORED

*NO, NOT THAT KIND.

WELCOME TO OUR ACTIVITY BOOK. WE HOPE THAT YOU ENJOY IT.

MAINLY BECAUSE WE WORKED LONG & HARD ON IT IN CHAIRS ALMOST AS OLD AS THE ONE BELOW.

BONUS FUN!
DRAW THE CORD AND
ACTUALLY PLUG HER
COMPUTER IN.

A QUICK NOTE BEFORE YOU START.

AKA: WE TRIED OUR BEST—BUT DON'T GET
MAD AT US IF WE MADE A MISTAKE.

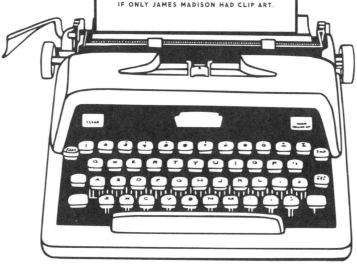

THIS BOOK IS JAMMED FULL OF FUN
(AND EXTREMELY RANDOM) ACTIVITIES,
GAMES, AND MINDLESS ENTERTAINMENT.
SO, WHILE WE TRIED REALLY HARD TO
MAKE SURE WE DIDN'T MAKE ANY ERRORS,
IT'S PROBABLY INEVITABLE. SORRY.

PLEASE DON'T YELL AT US. THIS IS AN
ACTIVITY BOOK, NOT THE CONSTITUTION.
BUT, COULD YOU IMAGINE IF THIS IS
WHAT THE CONSTITUTION LOOKED LIKE?
IF ONLY JAMES MADISON HAD CLIP ART.

A DOTS AND BOXES GAME SHEET

PSST: YOU'LL NEED A FRIEND (OR STRANGER) TO PLAY
THIS ONE WITH—OTHERWISE YOU'LL DEFINITELY WIN.

HOW TO PLAY

TWO PLAYERS TAKE TURNS ADDING A SINGLE HORIZONTAL OR VERTICAL LINE BETWEEN 2 UNJOINED
ADJACENT DOTS. A PLAYER WHO COMPLETES THE FOURTH SIDE OF A 1 BY 1 BOX EARNS ONE POINT
AND TAKES ANOTHER TURN (PLACING THEIR INITIAL INSIDE THE BOX). WHEN NO MORE PLAYS CAN BE
LEGALLY MADE, THE PLAYER WITH THE MOST POINTS IS DECLARED THE WINNER.

A SENSIBLE SEDAN COLORING SHEET

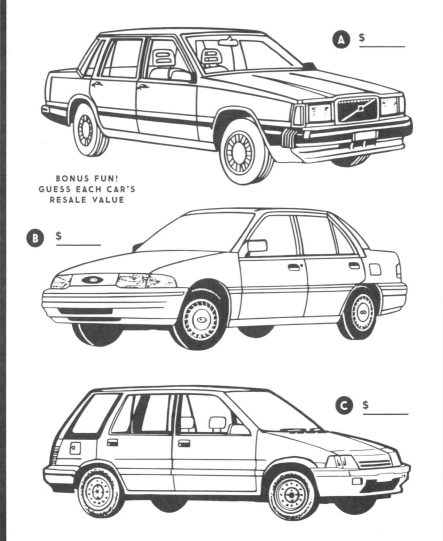

A $ _____

BONUS FUN!
GUESS EACH CAR'S
RESALE VALUE

B $ _____

C $ _____

5

```
F Y M R P F O S S T A C S X T L I F
A O T H A C S L O R G P R S C Y V A
N S O S H O W G I R L S Q J A O X J
T T B R R P C K N A M O W T A C Y A
A R V S P X C O C K T A I L T M T C
S I T H E E M O J I M O V I E S X K
T P H D I R T Y L O V E O U G A E A
I T E B A B B U W D G D M L B V L N
C E P O H W R R L R T E P T J I I D
F A O L U C E G H O S T S C A N S J
O S S E R N A I W L S I L G I G Z I
U E T R P K K T K N D B W T N C A L
R B M O S S I L S R T V A B E H I L
T G A S L U N I M F N G X R X R C N
V D N U R U G E V O L E H T J I B H
N S S T B W D N A F F W L O H S A L
M I J R D B A D L U V X C S E T N K
T R W I L D W I L D W E S T O M L A
X L V B J D N A S C V J D A Q A E X
I V H I Q V S W E P T A W A Y S B O
```

FIND THESE MOVIE TITLES

CATWOMAN
FANTASTIC FOUR
JACK AND JILL
STRIPTEASE
BOLERO
THE LOVE GURU

BREAKING DAWN
COCKTAIL
GHOST SCAN
SAVING CHRISTMAS
SWEPT AWAY
THE POSTMAN

THE EMOJI MOVIE
CATS
DIRTY LOVE
GIGLI
SHOWGIRLS
WILD WILD WEST

BONUS:

WHAT DO
THEY ALL
HAVE IN
COMMON?

SORRY FOR WHATEVER I SCREWED UP

HAVE YOU SEEN
THE PRICES OF
FLOWERS THESE
DAYS? APOLOGIZE
ON A BUDGET.

COLOR THESE
AND GIVE THEM
TO WHOEVER YOU
RECENTLY MADE
MAD INSTEAD.

START

FINISH

A SUDOKU PUZZLE ACTIVITY SHEET

A NUMBER PUZZLE THAT HAS ABSOLUTELY NOTHING
TO DO WITH NUMBERS—JUST THE WAY WE LIKE IT.

3		1	7				2	
				8		5		9
				4				7
			4	2		8		
7	4		1	3	6			
9		3	5		8		1	4
	9	4					7	
	8			1			9	
		5	6	9	7			1

HOW TO PLAY

JUST IN CASE YOU HAVE BEEN LOCKED AWAY IN A CULT FOR THE PAST TWENTY YEARS—SUDOKU IS
PLAYED ON A GRID OF 81 SPACES. WITHIN THIS ARE 9 'SQUARES' (EACH MADE OF A 3 BY 3 GRID).
EACH ROW, COLUMN, AND SQUARE MUST BE FILLED WITH THE NUMBERS 1-9, WITHOUT REPEATING
ANY NUMBERS WITHIN THE ROW, COLUMN, OR SQUARE. IT'S EASY—IN THEORY.

DRAW YOURSELF AS A PREDATORY LAWYER ON A BILLBOARD

DON'T FORGET A CATCHY PHONE NUMBER, SOMETHING LIKE 1-888-SO-SUE-ME.

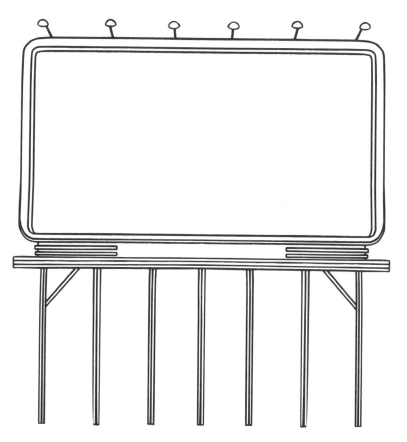

BLACK FRIDAY IN THE YEAR 2037
COLORING SHEET

FIND THESE WORDS

```
S U L E Z E X H Y Z P F Q X B U O N
F P H R X W H Y N O T R S B E T Z O
U G E P V B P G E S U C P C V T A B
U N C E R T A I N B X O P M R Q K B
T S C D D A T N O U Z C O J A K K Q
Q L H D I F F K G A Y A L I M M J O
S Q F U N N C N M S T J T G D G V L
A R N Y P H O U W I N N E B A G O M
B B A N H X M S V E E N M D Q O Q I
S K L V I O X Z A C N G Q E J B P D
O X X M G B D I A U S P T V O L S S
N B Y L Z E G L K H R E Z C G O W L
Q Z T X W L P B L C R O D Q Q N O R
I F L O J D A H Z C O B G C V G E P
J F R T L U I U N I V W O N B N R J
H J Y I G P E O N A T X A P J Z B S
X X J W E U C T P D A T Z R J S U A
R Q R P X S H U R T H X V O D W P K
N Z M E M R B B K V H O O K E R K J
C N D F A C A P I N K M E V L X Z S
```

BONUS: WHAT DO THEY ALL HAVE IN COMMON?

CONCRETE	COWARD	WINNEBAGO
FRIES	HOOKER	WHYNOT
OBLONG	OKAY	PINK
PLACENTIA	SPEED	UNCERTAIN
HURT	DINOSAUR	BANGS

CRACK THE CODE FOR AN IMPORTANT MESSAGE!

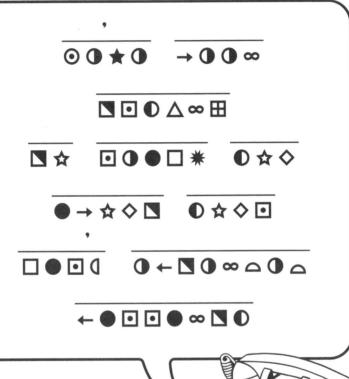

BONUS FUN: IDENTIFY THAT WEIRD LOOKING OBJECT TO THE RIGHT.

14

A FILL-IN-THE-BLANK STORY ACTIVITY SHEET

ANSWER THE QUESTIONS BELOW AND USE THEM TO
COMPLETE THE STORY ON THE NEXT PAGE.

1. NAME AN ACTIVITY THAT
   ENDS WITH 'ING'

2. NAME A PLURAL NOUN

3. NAME A VERB THAT
   ENDS WITH 'ING'

4. NAME A PAST-TENSE VERB

5. NAME AN ADJECTIVE

6. NAME AN ANIMAL OR PERSON

7. NAME A PAST-TENSE VERB

8. NAME AN ADJECTIVE

9. NAME AN ADJECTIVE

10. NAME A LOCATION

11. NAME A PLURAL TIME OF DAY

12. NAME A PLACE

13. NAME A BODY PART

14. NAME A PAST-TENSE VERB

15. NAME A NOUN

16. NAME AN ACTION VERB

BETTY LOU

BONUS FUN:
FEEL FREE TO DRAW
YOUR BEDROOM—THAT
SHE JUST SUDDENLY
APPEARED IN

A HAUNTED DOLL COLORING SHEET (AND ORIGIN STORY)

PSST: FLIP TO THE PREVIOUS PAGE AND FILL OUT THE QUESTIONS—NOW USE THEM TO COMPLETE THE STORY.

BETTY LOU LOVED 1_____ MORE THAN ANYTHING. THAT'S WHY SHE DECIDED TO IGNORE THE 2_____ AND KEEP 3_____ . SADLY, SHE WAS 4_____ BY A/AN 5_____ 6_____ AND HER SOUL WAS 7_____ INTO A 8_____ DOLL THAT JUST HAPPENED TO BE IN A/AN 9_____ 10_____ NEARBY. NOW SHE SPENDS HER 11_____ HAUNTING THE LOCAL 12_____ . SHE'S MOSTLY HARMLESS, JUST DON'T LOOK INTO HER 13_____ OR YOU'LL INSTANTLY BE 14_____ INTO A 15_____ THAT LOVES TO 16_____ .

```
C G B A Q D Q O S E A N B E A N C V
X P S A D A M W E S T I K R D X O J
D O M I N I C W E S T E J N T Z A A
G R E X H A R R I S O N E T T R V M
M T V U A R A L P H F I E N N E S E
H C A B X R U W B B R Q C B G V R S
C L A C G T Y W J F V X H I F G I M
S I J O S U E G T G T Z R L L M C A
A N W G P B Z R D U C S I V G I H S
M T E J G S E A O S D N S R C C A O
N E G W F P A Y M L O T T F N H R N
E A N B U D U B O L A X I Q K A D C
I S J R W M W N A B J W A R A E B A
L T K M W L Y I M L K V N B B L U R
L W Q O V E D V Q T V M B Y N C R Y
N O B O R L L E A N I W A A L A T G
K O V T A D T Q C S F R L P B I O R
K D R B W F C H E Z E Z E E Q N N A
X U V E P J L H L P H T N N Z E F N
B Y P L I A M N E E S O N L Q W Y T
```

FIND THESE ACTORS

ADAM WEST
CHRISTIAN BALE
JAMES MASON
RALPH FIENNES
RUPERT FRIEND

BURT REYNOLDS
CLINT EASTWOOD
LIAM NEESON
REX HARRISON
SAM NEILL

CARY GRANT
DOMINIC WEST
MICHAEL CAINE
RICHARD BURTON
SEAN BEAN

A CROWDED BAR COLORING SHEET

PICK ONE SONG TO PLAY THAT WILL
CLEAR OUT THE ENTIRE PLACE.

A WHAT'S NEW
PUSSYCAT?

TOM JONES

B MAMBO NO. 5

LOU BEGA

C CHRISTMAS
DON'T
BE LATE

THE CHIPMUNKS

D ALL STAR

SMASH MOUTH

E ACHY BREAKY
HEART

BILLY RAY CYRUS

F THONG SONG

SISQÓ

A MAKE-A-LIST ACTIVITY SHEET

A LIST OF THINGS TO BUY THE NEXT TIME
THAT I'M DRUNK AT A GROCERY STORE.

1 _____

2 _____

3 _____

4 _____

5 _____

6 _____

7 _____

8 _____

9 _____

10 _____

11 _____

12 _____

13 _____

14 _____

15 _____

16 _____

17 _____

18 _____

BONUS FUN:
WHY STOP AT 18?
FEEL FREE TO
USE SOME SCRAP
PAPER, TOO

A DOTS AND BOXES GAME SHEET

PSST: YOU'LL NEED A FRIEND (OR STRANGER) TO PLAY
THIS ONE WITH—OTHERWISE YOU'LL DEFINITELY WIN.

HOW TO PLAY

TWO PLAYERS TAKE TURNS ADDING A SINGLE HORIZONTAL OR VERTICAL LINE BETWEEN 2 UNJOINED
ADJACENT DOTS. A PLAYER WHO COMPLETES THE FOURTH SIDE OF A 1 BY 1 BOX EARNS ONE POINT
AND TAKES ANOTHER TURN (PLACING THEIR INITIAL INSIDE THE BOX). WHEN NO MORE PLAYS CAN BE
LEGALLY MADE, THE PLAYER WITH THE MOST POINTS IS DECLARED THE WINNER.

A PUNCTUALITY ACTIVITY SHEET

> DRAW IN THE CLOCK HANDS TO SHOW
> WHEN YOU'LL ACTUALLY ARRIVE.

**A FIRST DATE
AT 7:30 PM**

**A JOB INTERVIEW
AT 11:15 AM**

**A HAPPY HOUR
AT 5:00 PM ON
A FRIDAY**

**A FRIEND'S
'MOVING PARTY' AT 9:00 AM
ON A SATURDAY**

A SUDOKU PUZZLE ACTIVITY SHEET

A NUMBER PUZZLE THAT HAS ABSOLUTELY NOTHING
TO DO WITH NUMBERS—JUST THE WAY WE LIKE IT.

3		9	2	7	8		4	
				5				7
	8	4	3	1	6	2		
2	7	8		3	4	1		9
	6	1				4	5	
5						8		
6		5	7		2	9		8
	7	6		1				
4	1	2		8		5	7	6

HOW TO PLAY

JUST IN CASE YOU HAVE BEEN LOCKED AWAY IN A CULT FOR THE PAST TWENTY YEARS—SUDOKU IS
PLAYED ON A GRID OF 81 SPACES. WITHIN THIS ARE 9 'SQUARES' (EACH MADE OF A 3 BY 3 GRID).
EACH ROW, COLUMN, AND SQUARE MUST BE FILLED WITH THE NUMBERS 1-9, WITHOUT REPEATING
ANY NUMBERS WITHIN THE ROW, COLUMN, OR SQUARE. IT'S EASY—IN THEORY.

A STILL CLEAN CLOTHING STORAGE ACTIVITY SHEET

ESTIMATE HOW MANY ITEMS OF CLEAN CLOTHING
THAT EACH STORAGE SYSTEM WILL HOLD.

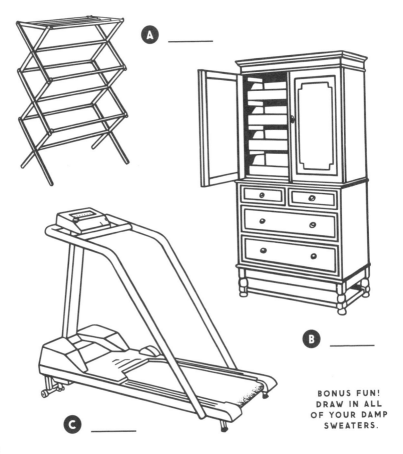

A _____

B _____

C _____

BONUS FUN!
DRAW IN ALL
OF YOUR DAMP
SWEATERS.

A MAKE-A-LIST ACTIVITY SHEET

> A RUNNING LIST OF THE REASONS THAT I
> SHOULDN'T EAT A SALAD FOR LUNCH.

1 _____

2 _____

3 _____

4 _____

5 _____

6 _____

7 _____

8 _____

9 _____

10 _____

11 _____

12 _____

13 _____

14 _____

15 _____

16 _____

17 _____

18 _____

BONUS FUN:
WHY STOP AT 18?
FEEL FREE TO
USE SOME SCRAP
PAPER, TOO

A BOTTOMLESS BLOODY MARY COLORING SHEET

BONUS: BE SURE TO ADD GARNISHES—LIKE A STICK OF CELERY OR AN ENTIRE ROTISSERIE CHICKEN.

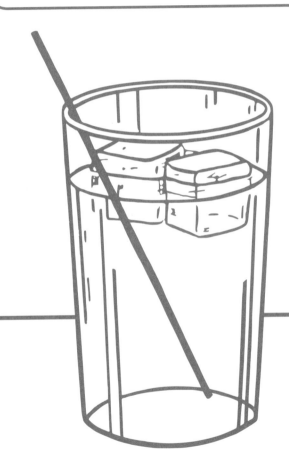

```
W C H X Q J J O H N G O O D M A N Y
S F H O V P N F K C V B H D S R E G
M C Z R A D L P X B K K D W R F C A
J I A N I G A M D Y B U K G A D A R
F D N R L S T N B Q R C V N Y A N U
D W J S L L T L X L H C I H Y N D W
R A O U R E A O U K S T T G I N I I
E Y H Q L P T A P D M R Q F W Y C L
W N N S Z E P T J H A D W W P D E L
B E M U M X C Y J C E Y G E R E B F
A J U A M A V L C O Z R G F D V E E
R O L G J L N M M L H N W P G I R R
R H A C H O A W Y E T A L A P T G R
Y N N Z A S N P Q U G O N Z L O E E
M S E K S E Y A S Q D L M S C K N L
O O Y I L Y P T H B S K A H S E E L
R N L H P P L V J H N P I A A O U N
E E D P L R M V V P I W G H S N N H
M S E E H O H F M M I L A T G E K B
F B I L L M U R R A Y S L H U N U S
```

FIND THESE CELEBRITIES

CHRISTOPHER WALKEN
MELISSA MCCARTHY
DREW BARRYMORE
SCARLETT JOHANSSON
DWAYNE JOHNSON

JOHN GOODMAN
CANDICE BERGEN
WILL FERREL
JOHN MULANEY
DANNY DEVITO

PAUL RUDD
BILL MURRAY
JONAH HILL
TINA FEY
TOM HANKS

A DOTS AND BOXES GAME SHEET

PSST: YOU'LL NEED A FRIEND (OR STRANGER) TO PLAY
THIS ONE WITH—OTHERWISE YOU'LL DEFINITELY WIN.

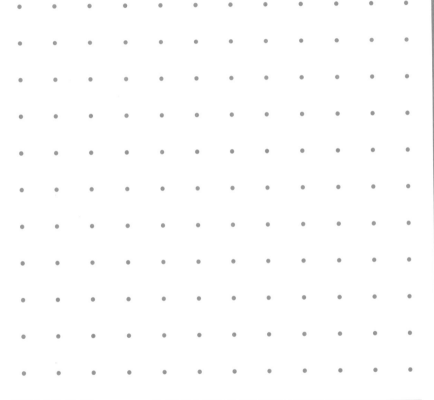

HOW TO PLAY

TWO PLAYERS TAKE TURNS ADDING A SINGLE HORIZONTAL OR VERTICAL LINE BETWEEN 2 UNJOINED
ADJACENT DOTS. A PLAYER WHO COMPLETES THE FOURTH SIDE OF A 1 BY 1 BOX EARNS ONE POINT
AND TAKES ANOTHER TURN (PLACING THEIR INITIAL INSIDE THE BOX). WHEN NO MORE PLAYS CAN BE
LEGALLY MADE, THE PLAYER WITH THE MOST POINTS IS DECLARED THE WINNER.

A FILL-IN-THE-BLANK STORY ACTIVITY SHEET

ANSWER THE QUESTIONS BELOW AND USE THEM TO COMPLETE THE STORY ON THE NEXT PAGE.

1. NAME AN ADJECTIVE

2. NAME A PAST-TENSE VERB

3. NAME A PAST-TENSE VERB

4. NAME A PAST-TENSE VERB

5. NAME A PLURAL NOUN

6. NAME AN ADJECTIVE

7. NAME A MONTH

8. NAME A PLACE

9. NAME A PAST-TENSE VERB

10. NAME AN ADJECTIVE

11. NAME A BODY PART

12. NAME A PAST-TENSE VERB

13. NAME A PLACE

14. NAME AN ADJECTIVE

15. NAME AN ACTION VERB

16. NAME A PLURAL ANIMAL

BLAIRE & CLAIRE

BONUS FUN:
ADD SOME SPEECH
BUBBLES WITH
WHATEVER THEY'RE
SAYING IN UNISON.

A HAUNTED DOLL COLORING SHEET (AND ORIGIN STORY)

PSST: FLIP TO THE PREVIOUS PAGE AND FILL OUT THE QUESTIONS—NOW USE THEM TO COMPLETE THE STORY.

GROWING UP AS <u>   1   </u> TWINS, BLAIRE & CLAIRE WERE INSEPARABLE. THEY DID EVERYTHING TOGETHER. THEY <u>   2   </u> TOGETHER, THEY <u>   3   </u> TOGETHER, THEY EVEN <u>   4   </u> <u>   5   </u> TOGETHER. THAT WAS UNTIL A/AN <u> 6 </u> <u> 7 </u> DAY WHEN THEY WERE AT THE LOCAL <u> 8 </u> AND BLAIRE ACCIDENTALLY <u> 9 </u> ON CLAIRE'S <u> 10 </u> <u> 11 </u> . CLAIRE WAS FURIOUS AND <u> 12 </u> HER SISTER INTO A <u> 13 </u> , INSTANTLY TURNING THEM BOTH INTO <u> 14 </u> DOLLS THAT HAUNT PEOPLE THAT <u> 15 </u> <u> 16 </u> .

```
T K C E C I L T U R T L E I J Y P K
Y E M M I C H I G A N J F R O G Q T
C O Z H N R W I E T G F G Z N B O V
K N G O I H Q O P M S K V I N G A A
B I F B T N R G I V C I U C A M B U
E N O K I U J M K U M G N O S N K C
A H X Z C C Q O D U N W K L T R E I
K J Y X T W W A Y E G W G O Y G G S
Y E K L Q S S C P G A W Q N C O V G
B B S V H S O Y O H A Q G E A S G O
U X O W I S O D Y D R Z B L N S A O
Z U X L Q B E R D S Y Y N S A A B F
Z V E A Y I E R Y J N J M H S M B Y
A M Q A L N A F L I L I P U T E Y G
R M L R E Y N W A H K C F F A R G O
D P A H N E G S K Q X Q V F B Q O P
M H L R L E V A R M A X B L L K A H
C Y A K X S S M H G Z L B E J E T E
W B A W I T C H H A Z E L P M Z S R
G H W T B B L A R L R X I R Y F O S
```

FIND THESE NAMES

BARNYARD DAWG

CHARLIE DOG

GABBY GOAT

HENERY HAWK

NASTY CANASTA

CECIL TURTLE

BEAKY BUZZARD

COLONEL SHUFFLE

GOOFY GOPHERS

MICHIGAN J FROG

PLAYBOY PENGUIN

MELISSA DUCK

GOSSAMER

WITCH HAZEL

FOXY

SNIFFLES

BONUS:
WHAT DO THEY ALL HAVE IN COMMON?

RATE DISGUSTING VEGETABLES ACTIVITY SHEET

WRITE IN THE INANIMATE OBJECT THAT YOU WOULD RATHER EAT THAN THE VEGETABLE.

A _____

_____ B

C _____

D _____

E _____

A MAKE-A-LIST ACTIVITY SHEET

THE DISADVANTAGES I'VE FACED DUE TO
BEING SO EXTREMELY ATTRACTIVE.

1 _____

2 _____

3 _____

4 _____

5 _____

6 _____

7 _____

8 _____

9 _____

10 _____

11 _____

12 _____

13 _____

14 _____

15 _____

16 _____

17 _____

18 _____

BONUS FUN:
WHY STOP AT 18?
FEEL FREE TO
USE SOME SCRAP
PAPER, TOO

START

FINISH

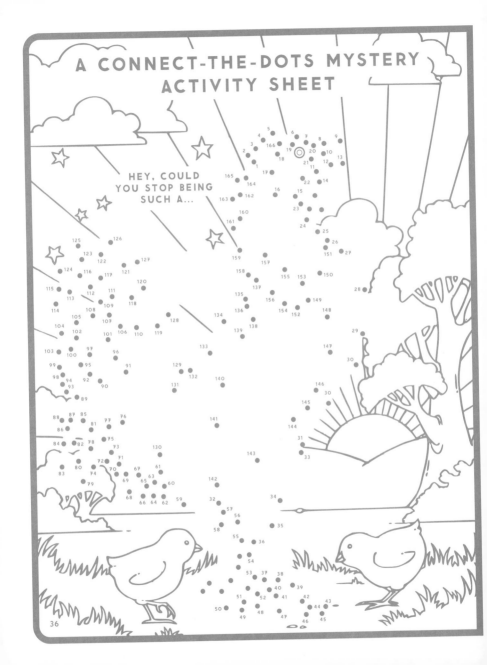

A MAJOR AWARD ACTIVITY SHEET

IT'S TIME THAT YOU FINALLY GIVE PEOPLE
THE RECOGNITION THAT THEY DESERVE.

PSST: FEEL FREE TO MAKE COPIES IF YOU PLAN
TO HOLD A FORMAL AWARD CEREMONY.

A BLACKOUT-DRUNK TATTOO ACTIVITY SHEET

YOU WOKE UP AFTER A NIGHT OF DRINKING
WITH THESE TATTOOS. RATE THEM.

A

BUDGET
UNICORN

___ /10

B

WILFORD BRIMLEY
AS A VIKING

___ /10

C

CROSS EYED WOLF

___ /10

SUGGESTIVE
FRUIT

___ /10

D

A DOTS AND BOXES GAME SHEET

PSST: YOU'LL NEED A FRIEND (OR STRANGER) TO PLAY THIS ONE WITH—OTHERWISE YOU'LL DEFINITELY WIN.

HOW TO PLAY

TWO PLAYERS TAKE TURNS ADDING A SINGLE HORIZONTAL OR VERTICAL LINE BETWEEN 2 UNJOINED ADJACENT DOTS. A PLAYER WHO COMPLETES THE FOURTH SIDE OF A 1 BY 1 BOX EARNS ONE POINT AND TAKES ANOTHER TURN (PLACING THEIR INITIAL INSIDE THE BOX). WHEN NO MORE PLAYS CAN BE LEGALLY MADE, THE PLAYER WITH THE MOST POINTS IS DECLARED THE WINNER.

```
P D P D E R E K H O U G H Y Q R I E
H A Q M D L L O X L J D M W T A A H
E N Y M R Z E Y V N F A I M P T G R
A N U L H L L V B U L D P P N D I T
T Y E T H H H D C L G M W O L X I Q
H F M R L A N C E A R M S T R O N G
L U C A H K A B B X R L A K P S O I
E J N H B E W T S S I E D S D X A Y
D I Z D R E G E Q W U M A P B P L W
G S W D H I V S N I K E M U X H E A
E A Z T N Q S E P G S S S S L J X R
R W T C A Y W R O J Y C C K X A R Z
R A F D N O A U O G F B O Z M L O L
M N L E B E M G I B W C T U T X D A
E A C E T R W J E B I H T B A P R M
L W I W K D H F U Y Q N X B E S I J
M D A X S H E P A R D I S F B A G G
U U N R K W H L S P F J J O W O U U
F Y N I C K J O N A S Z L A N X E B
F U S A Q B R U S G B X C O R K Z H
```

FIND THESE CELEBRITIES

ALEX RODRIGUEZ
DAX SHEPARD
HEATH LEDGER
DANNY FUJISAWA

CHRIS ROBINSON
DEREK HOUGH
LANCE ARMSTRONG
MATTHEW BELLAMY

OWEN WILSON
DIPLO
NICK JONAS
ADAM SCOTT

BONUS:
WHAT DO THEY ALL HAVE IN COMMON?

BRINGING WHITE BREAD TO A LAKE COLORING SHEET

A SUDOKU PUZZLE ACTIVITY SHEET

A NUMBER PUZZLE THAT HAS ABSOLUTELY NOTHING
TO DO WITH NUMBERS—JUST THE WAY WE LIKE IT.

1		4			8			
9		7		4	6	8		
2		3	9	7		6	5	4
		8		9				6
	4							
			1	2			8	
	3		4		5	7		
		2		3		4		
4	7						3	1

HOW TO PLAY

JUST IN CASE YOU HAVE BEEN LOCKED AWAY IN A CULT FOR THE PAST TWENTY YEARS—SUDOKU IS
PLAYED ON A GRID OF 81 SPACES. WITHIN THIS ARE 9 'SQUARES' (EACH MADE OF A 3 BY 3 GRID).
EACH ROW, COLUMN, AND SQUARE MUST BE FILLED WITH THE NUMBERS 1-9, WITHOUT REPEATING
ANY NUMBERS WITHIN THE ROW, COLUMN, OR SQUARE. IT'S EASY—IN THEORY.

A FILL-IN-THE-BLANK STORY ACTIVITY SHEET

ANSWER THE QUESTIONS BELOW AND USE THEM TO COMPLETE THE STORY ON THE NEXT PAGE.

1. NAME AN EMOTION

2. NAME AN ADJECTIVE

3. NAME AN ADJECTIVE

4. NAME A DAY OF THE WEEK

5. NAME AN ANIMAL OR PERSON

6. NAME A VERB THAT ENDS IN 'ING'

7. NAME AN ADJECTIVE

8. NAME AN ANIMAL OR PERSON

9. NAME AN ADJECTIVE

10. NAME A PAST-TENSE VERB

11. NAME AN ADJECTIVE

12. NAME AN ANIMAL OR PERSON

13. NAME A VERB THAT ENDS IN 'ING'

14. NAME A NOUN

15. NAME A PLACE

16. NAME AN ACTIVITY

CONSTANCE

BONUS FUN:
HELP COMPLETE
HER HAUNTED CROSS
STITCH-MAYBE
SOMETHING LIKE
'LIFE, LAUGH, LOOK
DEAD INSIDE'

A HAUNTED DOLL COLORING SHEET (AND ORIGIN STORY)

PSST: FLIP TO THE PREVIOUS PAGE AND FILL OUT THE QUESTIONS—NOW USE THEM TO COMPLETE THE STORY.

CONSTANCE LIVED A/AN $_1$_____ AND $_2$_____ LIFE. AT LEAST SHE DID, UNTIL THE $_3$_____ $_4$_____ THAT SHE ACCIDENTALLY SAW HER $_5$_____ $_6$_____ WITH A/AN $_7$_____ $_8$_____. IT WAS IMPOSSIBLE TO FORGET. EVENTUALLY, THE TRAUMA PROVED TO BE TOO $_9$_____, AND HER SOUL $_{10}$_____ INTO A/AN $_{11}$_____ DOLL. SADLY, THE FIRST THING SHE SAW WHILE IN HER NEW DOLL BODY WAS A/AN $_{12}$_____ REPEATEDLY $_{13}$_____ WITH A/AN $_{14}$_____. NOW SHE JUST ROAMS THE HALLS OF THE LOCAL $_{15}$_____ TRYING TO $_{16}$_____.

PICK ONLY ONE ITEM TO HAVE ON A DESERTED ISLAND

SLINGSHOT

ALCOHOL

MYSTERY JUG

VOLLEYBALL

MAGICAL T.V.

WHATEVER THIS IS

```
S M A R T Y J O N E S N A N Y Z R E
S A E A L W A Y S D R E A M I N G T
F E T H U N D E R G U L C H V U E Z
U X A E S I L V E R C H A R M J M F
S W I H J A E R N F G F C F R C O Z
A M H P E V G A C O B O C A O A G C
I K A G O R C K O P C R G S F N K O
C H L Y J A O N U L Q I R F M I I G
H C A L I F O R N I A C H R O M E V
I S E J X U U K T S E H B I S A A S
P B T Y Y Y J O R A R S A P A L U U
E K H R Z U M J Y S X T R L Y K T P
G P F C E O J P H D B R B A Y I H E
A C T Z C E N F O F P I A P V N E R
S I T A C F T Q U C G K R H F G N S
U M I G D A A S S R B E O S B D T A
S G D O D R J K E H R W L R N O I V
O G R I N D S T O N E J O A S M C E
F N R P Z N F W Y F S N Z O N P F R
R E A L Q U I E T B Q E K H M I O Q
```

FIND THESE PHRASES

GIACOMO
REAL QUIET
SILVER CHARM
ORB
SUPER SAVER
BARBARO

ANIMAL KINGDOM
CALIFORNIA CHROME
ALWAYS DREAMING
THUNDER GULCH
COUNTRY HOUSE
FUSAICHI PEGASUS

SEA HERO
STREET SENSE
AUTHENTIC
GRINDSTONE
RICH STRIKE
SMARTY JONES

A DOTS AND BOXES GAME SHEET

PSST: YOU'LL NEED A FRIEND (OR STRANGER) TO PLAY THIS ONE WITH—OTHERWISE YOU'LL DEFINITELY WIN.

HOW TO PLAY

TWO PLAYERS TAKE TURNS ADDING A SINGLE HORIZONTAL OR VERTICAL LINE BETWEEN 2 UNJOINED ADJACENT DOTS. A PLAYER WHO COMPLETES THE FOURTH SIDE OF A 1 BY 1 BOX EARNS ONE POINT AND TAKES ANOTHER TURN (PLACING THEIR INITIAL INSIDE THE BOX). WHEN NO MORE PLAYS CAN BE LEGALLY MADE, THE PLAYER WITH THE MOST POINTS IS DECLARED THE WINNER.

IMPROVE THE NATIONAL MONUMENT (STATUE OF LIBERTY EDITION)

BONUS FUN!
DRAW IN THE CITY
IT WOULD LIKELY
BE LOCATED IN.

THE STATUE OF LIBERTY

THE STATUE OF HERBAL TEA

COMPLETE THE DRAWING
TO HELP THIS RACCOON'S
DREAM COME TRUE.

A SUDOKU PUZZLE ACTIVITY SHEET

A NUMBER PUZZLE THAT HAS ABSOLUTELY NOTHING
TO DO WITH NUMBERS—JUST THE WAY WE LIKE IT.

				6		5	2	4
					4	8		9
		4	2		3		1	
				8				
3			6	4	1			2
4		6				1		3
5		1	3	7	6			8
		8	4	2	5	3		1

HOW TO PLAY

JUST IN CASE YOU HAVE BEEN LOCKED AWAY IN A CULT FOR THE PAST TWENTY YEARS—SUDOKU IS
PLAYED ON A GRID OF 81 SPACES. WITHIN THIS ARE 9 'SQUARES' (EACH MADE OF A 3 BY 3 GRID).
EACH ROW, COLUMN, AND SQUARE MUST BE FILLED WITH THE NUMBERS 1-9, WITHOUT REPEATING
ANY NUMBERS WITHIN THE ROW, COLUMN, OR SQUARE. IT'S EASY—IN THEORY.

A MAKE-A-LIST ACTIVITY SHEET

WAYS TO DISGUISE THAT I'M STILL WEARING
THE SAME CLOTHES AS YESTERDAY.

1 _____

2 _____

3 _____

4 _____

5 _____

6 _____

7 _____

8 _____

9 _____

10 _____

11 _____

12 _____

13 _____

14 _____

15 _____

16 _____

17 _____

18 _____

BONUS FUN:
WHY STOP AT 18?
FEEL FREE TO
USE SOME SCRAP
PAPER, TOO

A DOTS AND BOXES GAME SHEET

PSST: YOU'LL NEED A FRIEND (OR STRANGER) TO PLAY
THIS ONE WITH—OTHERWISE YOU'LL DEFINITELY WIN.

HOW TO PLAY

TWO PLAYERS TAKE TURNS ADDING A SINGLE HORIZONTAL OR VERTICAL LINE BETWEEN 2 UNJOINED
ADJACENT DOTS. A PLAYER WHO COMPLETES THE FOURTH SIDE OF A 1 BY 1 BOX EARNS ONE POINT
AND TAKES ANOTHER TURN (PLACING THEIR INITIAL INSIDE THE BOX). WHEN NO MORE PLAYS CAN BE
LEGALLY MADE, THE PLAYER WITH THE MOST POINTS IS DECLARED THE WINNER.

```
C G G N P Q Z D O Q Y Y P V E U L S
A I C O I U J R A S R U J L N G R Z
S L O V X R Y U E Q Q A L G T U Q S
U A C H Q O G G V X C A E P O I E T
A U K G S M Z T E K C X Y H C C C Y
L N T O Y L J E I E B D R R N T A M
F C A P G V Q S R E A E Y A C H S K
R H I Z E A T T M K T W L V O E I K
I P L F L W C I N F Q L V O M S N W
D A S R T U O N A I I R X Y P T O C
A R O R D W E G J E I G B I A I N H
Y T I O B K R D V F P K W L N N I A
K Y R C N S K R A M Y F N A Y G G I
R P Q F F U U F J K F S K M P B H R
V P Y U Q S O Z Q E T S S W I H T M
N E Y I L T H E C A R P E T C T J O
T K J I B S W J O B F A I R N W N D
G B A S K E T B A L L J R H I C H E
Q M K S K A V F N Y D D B T C R S L
E M Q R S U I T W A R E H O U S E A
```

FIND THESE PHRASES

AFTER HOURS
CASUAL FRIDAY
COMPANY PICNIC
JOB FAIR
COCKTAILS

BASKETBALL
CHAIR MODEL
DRUG TESTING
LAUNCH PARTY
THE CARPET

CASINO NIGHT
SUIT WAREHOUSE
EMAIL SURVEILLANCE
PRODUCT RECALL
THE STING

BONUS:
WHAT DO
THEY ALL
HAVE IN
COMMON?

A FILL-IN-THE-BLANK STORY ACTIVITY SHEET

ANSWER THE QUESTIONS BELOW AND USE THEM TO COMPLETE THE STORY ON THE NEXT PAGE.

1. NAME A YEAR

2. NAME A VERB THAT ENDS IN 'ING'

3. NAME AN ADVERB

4. NAME AN ACTION VERB

5. NAME A PLURAL NOUN

6. NAME A PLURAL NOUN

7. NAME A NOUN

8. NAME A GROUP OF ANIMALS

9. NAME AN ACTION VERB

10. NAME A BODY PART

11. NAME AN ADJECTIVE

12. NAME A PAST-TENSE VERB

13. NAME AN ADJECTIVE

14. NAME AN ADJECTIVE

15. NAME A MAGAZINE

16. NAME A NOUN

GERTRUDE

BONUS FUN:
FINISH THE RANSOM
LETTER THAT SHE IS
WRITING TO CINDY

58

A HAUNTED DOLL COLORING SHEET (AND ORIGIN STORY)

PSST: FLIP TO THE PREVIOUS PAGE AND FILL OUT THE QUESTIONS—NOW USE THEM TO COMPLETE THE STORY.

DESPITE BEING BORN IN 1_____ ,
GERTRUDE INSISTED ON 2_____ WITH
QUILL PENS. MAINLY BECAUSE
SHE LOVED TO 3_____ 4_____ THE
5_____ OUT OF LIVE 6_____ .
SHE WAS KIND OF A/AN 7_____ , SO
SHE REALLY DESERVED IT WHEN
THE 8_____ DECIDED TO 9_____
AT HER 10_____ UNTIL SHE 11_____ .
AND IF THAT WASN'T ENOUGH, HER
12_____ SOUL WAS THEN TRANSFERED
INTO A/AN 13_____ DOLL AND SHE
WAS FORCED TO WRITE 14_____
POEMS FOR 15_____ WITH A 16_____ ,
DESPITE NOW BEING ALLERGIC.

A SUDOKU PUZZLE ACTIVITY SHEET

A NUMBER PUZZLE THAT HAS ABSOLUTELY NOTHING
TO DO WITH NUMBERS—JUST THE WAY WE LIKE IT.

	9	6	4		8	1		
	8	4	6					
	2			7			6	
6		8		9	2	4		
		5	7	1	4	6		8
		9	5	8		2	3	
9			2	4	3	7	8	
		7			9		1	2
8		2	1		7			3

HOW TO PLAY

JUST IN CASE YOU HAVE BEEN LOCKED AWAY IN A CULT FOR THE PAST TWENTY YEARS—SUDOKU IS
PLAYED ON A GRID OF 81 SPACES. WITHIN THIS ARE 9 'SQUARES' (EACH MADE OF A 3 BY 3 GRID).
EACH ROW, COLUMN, AND SQUARE MUST BE FILLED WITH THE NUMBERS 1-9, WITHOUT REPEATING
ANY NUMBERS WITHIN THE ROW, COLUMN, OR SQUARE. IT'S EASY—IN THEORY.

60

DROPPING A TOOL ON YOUR FOOT ACTIVITY SHEET

WRITE IN YOUR SWEAR WORD OF CHOICE AFTER EACH OBJECT LANDS ON YOUR BIG TOE

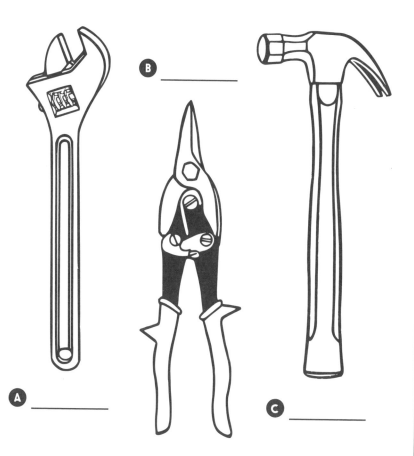

B _____

A _____

C _____

A MAKE-A-LIST ACTIVITY SHEET

A LIST OF THE DISEASES THAT I PROBABLY
HAVE ACCORDING TO THE INTERNET.

1 _____

2 _____

3 _____

4 _____

5 _____

6 _____

7 _____

8 _____

9 _____

10 _____

11 _____

12 _____

13 _____

14 _____

15 _____

16 _____

17 _____

18 _____

BONUS FUN:
WHY STOP AT 18?
FEEL FREE TO
USE SOME SCRAP
PAPER, TOO

A DOTS AND BOXES GAME SHEET

PSST: YOU'LL NEED A FRIEND (OR STRANGER) TO PLAY THIS ONE WITH—OTHERWISE YOU'LL DEFINITELY WIN.

HOW TO PLAY

TWO PLAYERS TAKE TURNS ADDING A SINGLE HORIZONTAL OR VERTICAL LINE BETWEEN 2 UNJOINED ADJACENT DOTS. A PLAYER WHO COMPLETES THE FOURTH SIDE OF A 1 BY 1 BOX EARNS ONE POINT AND TAKES ANOTHER TURN (PLACING THEIR INITIAL INSIDE THE BOX). WHEN NO MORE PLAYS CAN BE LEGALLY MADE, THE PLAYER WITH THE MOST POINTS IS DECLARED THE WINNER.

A CONNECT-THE-DOTS MYSTERY ACTIVITY SHEET

BONUS FUN:
FILL IN WHAT IS
DEAD TO YOU

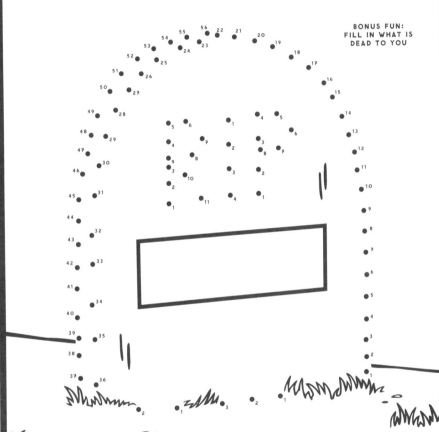

64

```
M W J K W F H U R L I N G D P H O P
Y Z Y C J N V P G L I M A N M H S E
W A R C D Q O Y B V X S E H D G R S
K W A T E R S K I I N G F X K L B A
N K L Z Q N Q L V Y M I R Y I I J P
F R O L L E R H O C K E Y F T D L A
R E B R E L O B A N D Y J L E I S L
B V O P F Z H U A C J M G Z F N F L
K Z U S M B G D Q L S A O P L G A O
R Y L F Z D A O Z N L U M D Y P V U
D N E V L Y V L B X X O H U I F U E
M N S L E Z Z F L T F L O O N B O T
A G T E N P I N B O W L I N G P V G
V N Q Z O G L B Q V J M Q U I D H X
H D G Q B U C G K C W Y T O X N F T
K L Y L M W P D C K E J A R U J G G
J T A S I P I G E O N R A C I N G V
S R U E E N S Z T H F G D B E N K F
S I E O I M G Z X R Y A E T D T V X
N S K I B A L L E T R J V H N I W E
```

FIND THESE ACTIVITIES

BONUS:
WHAT DO THEY ALL HAVE IN COMMON?

ANGLING
BANDY
KORFBALL
GLIDING

BOULES
BUDO
GLIMA
HURLING

WATER SKIING
ROLLER HOCKEY
TENPIN BOWLING
PIGEON RACING

KITE FLYING
PESAPALLO
BALLOONING
SKI BALLET

PICK THE BETTER HORSE NAME

LONG RANDY / BAMBINO

COWBOY / HOT WHEELS

GOOD INTENTIONS / DRILLBIT

MR. BIG MONEY / JERICHO

BUTTER / INDIANA MONTGOMERY

NOBLE STEP / LANDSLIDE

A MAKE-A-LIST ACTIVITY SHEET

A RUNNING LIST OF THE WORST IDEAS
FOR 'SEXY' HALLOWEEN COSTUMES.

1 _____

2 _____

3 _____

4 _____

5 _____

6 _____

7 _____

8 _____

9 _____

10 _____

11 _____

12 _____

13 _____

14 _____

15 _____

16 _____

17 _____

18 _____

BONUS FUN:
WHY STOP AT 18?
FEEL FREE TO
USE SOME SCRAP
PAPER, TOO

A DOTS AND BOXES GAME SHEET

PSST: YOU'LL NEED A FRIEND (OR STRANGER) TO PLAY THIS ONE WITH—OTHERWISE YOU'LL DEFINITELY WIN.

HOW TO PLAY

TWO PLAYERS TAKE TURNS ADDING A SINGLE HORIZONTAL OR VERTICAL LINE BETWEEN 2 UNJOINED ADJACENT DOTS. A PLAYER WHO COMPLETES THE FOURTH SIDE OF A 1 BY 1 BOX EARNS ONE POINT AND TAKES ANOTHER TURN (PLACING THEIR INITIAL INSIDE THE BOX). WHEN NO MORE PLAYS CAN BE LEGALLY MADE, THE PLAYER WITH THE MOST POINTS IS DECLARED THE WINNER.

WOMEN READING THEIR MESSAGES ON A DATING APP COLORING SHEET

```
P F K W A U Y G U F I M K U M S X P
D W P V B G G E D L O L D L Y M E I
I O S E E D E J A B U K Q L E E G E
C O Z Y C O R N E R I A F I R G N H
R T S Q B R E A D L O A F T Q F I O
O K A B Q H A P P Y L A N D I C R M
L Q T A Z Y H G M M P I M M F V Y Z
D W A L K C P N U O A H O B R C L B
F E N D B N P F H R S X S U I S C E
U G S H L Z H W B W E S Q Z E K E L
R Y K E I C I V G W N Z U R N X M C
N Q I A S J K Y F K J T I P D I J H
A V N D S J G O D A P E T J S O P E
C Z G Z C T O L R E W A O N H K D R
E K D I O O A Y A H J T V G I W S T
V U O C R P G K M B W I I O P J U O
T Q M I N S N G J F M C L V S Q J W
X C I K E H Y M H L X K L H X H Y N
Q T A Q R A Q U O W I E E R T Z S Y
N W C H P M B X E N Z T U R X X Z E
```

FIND THESE PHRASES

BALD HEAD

BRAINTREE

FRIENDSHIP

MOSSUP

SATAN'S KINGDOM

BELCHER TOWN

BREAD LOAF

HAPPYLAND

OLD FURNACE

TEATICKET

BLISS CORNER

COZY CORNER

MOSQUITOVILLE

OLD LYME

TOPSHAM

A FILL-IN-THE-BLANK STORY ACTIVITY SHEET

ANSWER THE QUESTIONS BELOW AND USE THEM TO COMPLETE THE STORY ON THE NEXT PAGE.

1. NAME A DECADE

2. NAME AN ADJECTIVE

3. NAME AN ADJECTIVE

4. NAME A PLURAL GROUP OF PEOPLE

5. NAME AN ACTION VERB

6. NAME AN OBJECT

7. NAME AN ADJECTIVE

8. NAME AN OBJECT

9. NAME A DAY OF THE WEEK

10. NAME A PAST-TENSE VERB

11. NAME AN ADJECTIVE

12. NAME AN ANIMAL OR PERSON

13. NAME AN ADJECTIVE

14. NAME A PLURAL PLACE

BEATRICE

BONUS FUN:
DRAW IN SOME TOYS
THAT WOULD BE EVEN
MORE FUN TO PLAY
WITH—LIKE A ROCK
OR SOMETHING.

A HAUNTED DOLL COLORING SHEET (AND ORIGIN STORY)

PSST: FLIP TO THE PREVIOUS PAGE AND FILL OUT THE QUESTIONS—NOW USE THEM TO COMPLETE THE STORY.

THE __1_____ WERE A/AN __2____ TIME TO BE ALIVE. A/AN __3____ GAME WAS POPULAR WITH THE LOCAL __4_____ CALLED HOOP AND STICK. BEATRICE COULD HARDLY __5_____ AT NIGHT, SHE JUST COULDN'T WAIT TO WAKE UP AND HIT THAT __6____ WITH HER __7_____ __8_____ . MAYBE SHE WAS DOING IT WRONG, BUT SHE DIDN'T CARE. ONE __9_____ THOUGH, EVERYTHING CHANGED WHEN SHE WAS TRAGICALLY __10_____ BY A/AN __11_____ __12_____ , TURNING HER INTO A/AN __13_____ DOLL. NOW SHE SEEKS REVENGE BY HAUNTING __14_____ .

A MAKE-A-LIST ACTIVITY SHEET

A CONVENIENT LIST OF ALL THE REASONS
THAT I'M UNFIT FOR JURY DUTY.

1 _____

2 _____

3 _____

4 _____

5 _____

6 _____

7 _____

8 _____

9 _____

10 _____

11 _____

12 _____

13 _____

14 _____

15 _____

16 _____

17 _____

18 _____

BONUS FUN:
WHY STOP AT 18?
FEEL FREE TO
USE SOME SCRAP
PAPER, TOO

A VEGAS CASINO ACTIVITY SHEET

SMOKE A PACK OF MENTHOLS,* STARE AT
THIS FOR 5 HOURS, AND TEAR UP $200.

*DON'T
ACTUALLY
SMOKE.

```
M W Z X U J G Z F N S R H U G O T Y
O K T I T N N M U C O S Y I O B B W
V D V Y G L N S Y U U V B I I U O S
C F T H E D A R K K N I G H T X H A
X A X I B I A E A W D Z O C P K E Q
H I U C M A N D Z N O O U B L U M C
K U K Q J R N C Q X F X Q X U L I O
A R C T P H Y M E W M K Q Y H O A E
R Y I K B D Y H R P E N R W U J N N
R W Q B T H E H U R T L O C K E R R
I X R N O R T H Y G A I K B N M H G
V F Q D C K U A C V L A O C V R A R
A H C J I X U I Z X S J H N H U P A
L F O R D V F E R R A R I H S B S V
K Y P L E R C W B C F D U N E B O I
X X N B S R Z X W H I P L A S H D T
T M A D M A X F U R Y R O A D M Y Y
R F Z Z U Y Z J O F A F R W L S G W
Q I L I O I Z Q K S K Y F A L L O G
C H D K D U N K I R K Y D M Q Q E V
```

FIND THESE MOVIES

ARRIVAL
DUNKIRK
HUGO
SKYFALL
DUNE
GRAVITY

BOHEMIAN RHAPSODY
FORD V FERRARI
INCEPTION
SOUND OF METAL
WHIPLASH
THE HURT LOCKER

MAD MAX FURY ROAD
THE DARK KNIGHT

BONUS:
WHAT DO THEY ALL HAVE IN COMMON?

A SUDOKU PUZZLE ACTIVITY SHEET

A NUMBER PUZZLE THAT HAS ABSOLUTELY NOTHING TO DO WITH NUMBERS—JUST THE WAY WE LIKE IT.

						9	2	6
6		9		2	1	8	7	
2	8		9	6	7	1	3	4
	2		4				8	7
								3
	6		7	9	5	2	4	
		8		7		4		
4		6		8	3	7	1	2
7	1				9	3	5	8

HOW TO PLAY

JUST IN CASE YOU HAVE BEEN LOCKED AWAY IN A CULT FOR THE PAST TWENTY YEARS—SUDOKU IS PLAYED ON A GRID OF 81 SPACES. WITHIN THIS ARE 9 'SQUARES' (EACH MADE OF A 3 BY 3 GRID). EACH ROW, COLUMN, AND SQUARE MUST BE FILLED WITH THE NUMBERS 1-9, WITHOUT REPEATING ANY NUMBERS WITHIN THE ROW, COLUMN, OR SQUARE. IT'S EASY—IN THEORY.

A DOTS AND BOXES GAME SHEET

PSST: YOU'LL NEED A FRIEND (OR STRANGER) TO PLAY THIS ONE WITH—OTHERWISE YOU'LL DEFINITELY WIN.

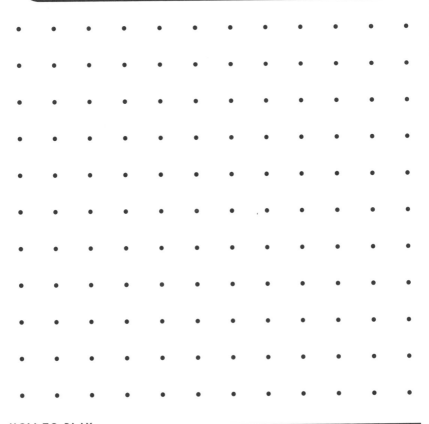

HOW TO PLAY

TWO PLAYERS TAKE TURNS ADDING A SINGLE HORIZONTAL OR VERTICAL LINE BETWEEN 2 UNJOINED ADJACENT DOTS. A PLAYER WHO COMPLETES THE FOURTH SIDE OF A 1 BY 1 BOX EARNS ONE POINT AND TAKES ANOTHER TURN (PLACING THEIR INITIAL INSIDE THE BOX). WHEN NO MORE PLAYS CAN BE LEGALLY MADE, THE PLAYER WITH THE MOST POINTS IS DECLARED THE WINNER.

WHAT IS THIS BIRD THINKING?

ADD IN ITS INNER DIALOGUE WHILE IT'S JUST
STANDING THERE—SILENTLY JUDGING YOU.

WORKING ON A GROUP PROJECT
COLORING SHEET

A SUDOKU PUZZLE ACTIVITY SHEET

A NUMBER PUZZLE THAT HAS ABSOLUTELY NOTHING
TO DO WITH NUMBERS—JUST THE WAY WE LIKE IT.

	7					9	2	6
2	3		1			5		7
9	5							
7		9					6	5
			7				8	1
1	8			6	5	7		3
		8		7		3		9
4			8		1	6		2
5	2	7	9		6	8		

HOW TO PLAY

JUST IN CASE YOU HAVE BEEN LOCKED AWAY IN A CULT FOR THE PAST TWENTY YEARS—SUDOKU IS
PLAYED ON A GRID OF 81 SPACES. WITHIN THIS ARE 9 'SQUARES' (EACH MADE OF A 3 BY 3 GRID).
EACH ROW, COLUMN, AND SQUARE MUST BE FILLED WITH THE NUMBERS 1-9, WITHOUT REPEATING
ANY NUMBERS WITHIN THE ROW, COLUMN, OR SQUARE. IT'S EASY—IN THEORY.

A FILL-IN-THE-BLANK STORY ACTIVITY SHEET

ANSWER THE QUESTIONS BELOW AND USE THEM TO COMPLETE THE STORY ON THE NEXT PAGE.

1. NAME AN ACTION VERB

2. NAME AN ADJECTIVE

3. NAME A YEAR

4. NAME AN ADJECTIVE

5. NAME AN ADJECTIVE

6. NAME AN OCCUPATION

7. NAME A PLURAL GROUP OF PEOPLE

8. NAME A PLURAL NOUN

9. NAME AN ADJECTIVE

10. NAME A PLURAL GROUP OF PEOPLE

11. NAME AN ACTION VERB

12. NAME A PLACE

13. NAME A NOUN

14. NAME A NOUN

LORETTA

A HAUNTED DOLL COLORING SHEET (AND ORIGIN STORY)

> PSST: FLIP TO THE PREVIOUS PAGE AND FILL OUT THE QUESTIONS—NOW USE THEM TO COMPLETE THE STORY.

LORETTA HAD ALWAYS BEEN ABLE TO _1_____ THE FUTURE. EVEN AT A/AN _2_____ AGE, SHE KNEW THAT IN _3_____ SHE'D BE TURNED INTO A/AN _4_____ DOLL BY A/AN _5_____ _6_____ . SHE EVEN TRIED TO WARN HER _7_____ , BUT THEY ALL ACTED LIKE _8_____ AND REFUSED TO HELP. THAT'S WHY, NOW STUCK INSIDE OF HER NEW _9_____ BODY, SHE LIKES TO SUDDENLY APPEAR IN FRONT OF _10_____ WHILE THEY'RE TRYING TO _11_____ AT THE LOCAL _12_____ AND YELL '_13_____ !' IT REALLY SCARES THE _14_____ OUT OF THEM.

A MAKE-A-LIST ACTIVITY SHEET

PEOPLE THAT SHARE MY BIRTHDAY,
RANKED FROM BEST TO WORST.

1 _____

2 _____

3 _____

4 _____

5 _____

6 _____

7 _____

8 _____

9 _____

10 _____

11 _____

12 _____

13 _____

14 _____

15 _____

16 _____

17 _____

18 _____

BONUS FUN:
WHY STOP AT 18?
FEEL FREE TO
USE SOME SCRAP
PAPER, TOO

```
D Z W Q N W E M F J M Z Z K G J A Q
B L A K M I S P S N O C D H E P T X
F Z Y H E N A K L S Z Y Y N O S D W
H I N L G R H B R Y P P Z K R R H X
A E E O A G C K Y M J L A Q G J Y E
F S B E N E Y Y X C T R J Y E K T E
I E R K M W V E D E Y E N D L C R N
T N A A U O E M N N R H E A O I O R
A C D R L Y H S A W A C L U P N H U
L R Y D L Y C F R A B S L W E N S O
N E R A A L Z O B Z A E A A Z O N B
E N L S L W S Y L N N R Y N O C I S
E N I H L P C X L A K D L D A Y T O
U E T I Y M D A E D S N I A X R R N
Q J A A W L I N S Y T A L S C R A O
U S N N U I C A S N K R K Y Q A M R
I I L J O D B E U O S F E K H H J A
K R Z U Z D K J R T V U X E J U J H
H K X T S P P I L I H P Y S U B N S
U O M F V V O A L A N T H I C K E U
```

FIND THESE CELEBRITIES

ALAN THICKE
FRAN DRESCHER
KRIS JENNER
RUSSELL BRAND
TYRA BANKS
WAYNE BRADY

BUSY PHILIPPS
SHARON OSBOURNE
GEORGE LOPEZ
MEGAN MULLALLY
WANDA SYKES
MARTIN SHORT

CHEVY CHASE
KHLOE KARDASHIAN
TONY DANZA
QUEEN LATIFAH
LILY ALLEN
HARRY CONNICK JR.

A DOTS AND BOXES GAME SHEET

PSST: YOU'LL NEED A FRIEND (OR STRANGER) TO PLAY THIS ONE WITH—OTHERWISE YOU'LL DEFINITELY WIN.

HOW TO PLAY

TWO PLAYERS TAKE TURNS ADDING A SINGLE HORIZONTAL OR VERTICAL LINE BETWEEN 2 UNJOINED ADJACENT DOTS. A PLAYER WHO COMPLETES THE FOURTH SIDE OF A 1 BY 1 BOX EARNS ONE POINT AND TAKES ANOTHER TURN (PLACING THEIR INITIAL INSIDE THE BOX). WHEN NO MORE PLAYS CAN BE LEGALLY MADE, THE PLAYER WITH THE MOST POINTS IS DECLARED THE WINNER.

REALLY OUTDATED TECHNOLOGY COLORING SHEET

_____

_____

BONUS FUN!
IDENTIFY WHAT
THESE MYSTERIOUS
OBJECTS DID

_____

_____

_____

_____

```
M I N K A K E L L Y A Z E U R D B C
K R I S T I N C A V A L L A R I S P
J J H Q X J U B B I W X H D W L K I
P E Q J E S S I C A S I M P S O N R
R P N E T K A T Y P E R R Y K Q J X
B R A N G R Z U Q M H F U O H J U A
V P E G I T T A Y L O R S W I F T L
A O C N X F R A S H I D A J O N E S
N W L L E D E H T F T G D Z M G B C
E I Y V A E L R O G O X I P N E O A
S E Q V X I Z W L N Z F H A H Q Y M
S H S S V F T E G O A A U W E J E E
A T W M U R A G L H V M N W L W I R
C D M E X N Q D T L Q E I D M U S O
A X A Y S Q D S I A W V H T V X D N
R A B V V H S D W N S E L E R X W D
L J S S U U S F J C Z V G V W A I I
T I R B H A T X L F L C S E W I M A
O F R T C F A Z O K Q V V U R H T Z
N J E N N I F E R A N I S T O N S T
```

FIND THESE CELEBRITIES

CAMERON DIAZ
JESSICA SIMPSON
MINKA KELLY
RHONA MITRA
KATY PERRY
RASHIDA JONES

JENNIFER ANISTON
TAYLOR SWIFT
JENNIFER LOVE HEWITT
KRISTIN CAVALLARI
RENEE ZELLWEGER
VANESSA CARLTON

BONUS:
WHAT DO THEY ALL HAVE IN COMMON?

ACCIDENTALLY TOUCHING A WORM COLORING SHEET

A SUDOKU PUZZLE ACTIVITY SHEET

A NUMBER PUZZLE THAT HAS ABSOLUTELY NOTHING
TO DO WITH NUMBERS—JUST THE WAY WE LIKE IT.

4			7		6			
3	5			2		6		7
		6	5		1		3	8
			6	5	3	8	7	2
8			1	7	9			4
7	6			8	2			9
5	1		9	6		7		
6		7	2			9	8	1
	8		3		7		5	6

HOW TO PLAY

JUST IN CASE YOU HAVE BEEN LOCKED AWAY IN A CULT FOR THE PAST TWENTY YEARS—SUDOKU IS
PLAYED ON A GRID OF 81 SPACES. WITHIN THIS ARE 9 'SQUARES' (EACH MADE OF A 3 BY 3 GRID).
EACH ROW, COLUMN, AND SQUARE MUST BE FILLED WITH THE NUMBERS 1-9, WITHOUT REPEATING
ANY NUMBERS WITHIN THE ROW, COLUMN, OR SQUARE. IT'S EASY—IN THEORY.

START

FINISH

A MAKE-A-LIST ACTIVITY SHEET

TORTURES THAT ARE STILL LIKELY BETTER
THAN HAVING A ROOMMATE.

1 _____

2 _____

3 _____

4 _____

5 _____

6 _____

7 _____

8 _____

9 _____

10 _____

11 _____

12 _____

13 _____

14 _____

15 _____

16 _____

17 _____

18 _____

BONUS FUN:
WHY STOP AT 18?
FEEL FREE TO
USE SOME SCRAP
PAPER, TOO

N H X Y H Y A G J W F O R Y O U A E
T J J W Q D B R K R T S T N O Q E N
L H S B A T M A N X I L H T U Z P C
F U E Q N X I F D U K T E V G U F H
K Z U R U W L F F V I T G Y P O I A
D D R O A X C I W O I P O C Y P C O
Q J Q C L I M T E K Q L L R Y K L S
W C W C P O N I T C E I D Y A I N A
L O B H M A M B T Z M R E S P V Y N
J N P H H D J R O R A T X T K O D D
H T L W N I L I B W N A P A A B O D
A R A P A R A D E N C G E L N Q O I
V O N B L T V G R B I H R B Y Y F S
K V E M V Y A E J L P Q I A A Q U O
I E T I Q M H H U X A H E L F L K R
D R E J U I N I G K T Q N L D D B D
Q S A O J N T X M Q I D C J E R I E
E Y R O X D O T F R O V E G Q I E R
S S T F C U M M K N J L U P K T N
L D H T H E B L A C K A L B U M C E

FIND THESE PHRASES

FOR YOU
BATMAN
DIRTY MIND
PARADE

CHAOS AND DISORDER
THE RAINBOW CHILDREN
THE BLACK ALBUM
THE GOLD EXPERIENCE

CONTROVERSY
EMANCIPATION
GRAFFITI BRIDGE
PLANET EARTH
CRYSTAL BALL

AN ACTUAL ADULT'S REFRIGERATOR ACTIVITY SHEET

PRETEND TO BE A RESPONSIBLE GROWN-UP AND FILL THIS WITH THEIR RIDICULOUS FOODS.

HINT:
START WITH
SOME KALE.

A FILL-IN-THE-BLANK STORY ACTIVITY SHEET

ANSWER THE QUESTIONS BELOW AND USE THEM TO COMPLETE THE STORY ON THE NEXT PAGE.

1. NAME AN EMOTION

2. NAME AN ACTION VERB

3. NAME AN ADJECTIVE

4. NAME AN ITEM OF CLOTHING

5. NAME A PLURAL NOUN

6. NAME A NOUN

7. NAME AN ADJECTIVE

8. NAME A NOUN

9. NAME A NOUN

10. NAME AN ADJECTIVE

11. NAME AN ACTION VERB

12. NAME AN ADJECTIVE

13. NAME A PLURAL PLACE

14. NAME AN ADJECTIVE

15. NAME AN ADJECTIVE

16. NAME AN ANIMAL OR PERSON

WILHELMINA

BONUS FUN:
DRAW HER HIDING
IN THE CURTAINS
THAT SHE CLEARLY
MADE HER DRESS
FROM

A HAUNTED DOLL COLORING SHEET (AND ORIGIN STORY)

PSST: FLIP TO THE PREVIOUS PAGE AND FILL OUT THE QUESTIONS—NOW USE THEM TO COMPLETE THE STORY.

THE RAIN REALLY MADE WILHELMINA
<u>1_____</u> . SHE WOULD <u>2_____</u> HER
FAVORITE <u>3_____</u> <u>4_____</u> , GRAB
HER UMBRELLA, AND HEAD OUTSIDE
TO SPLASH IN THE <u>5_____</u> .
UNFORTUNATELY HER UMBRELLA WAS
MADE OF <u>6_____</u> , SO IT WAS JUST
A MATTER OF TIME UNTIL IT WAS
STRUCK BY A/AN <u>7_____</u> <u>8_____</u> .
INSTANTLY THE <u>9_____</u> TURNED HER
INTO A/AN <u>10_____</u> DOLL, FOREVER
CURSED TO <u>11_____</u> ALL OF THE
<u>12_____</u> <u>13_____</u> ACROSS THE GLOBE.
WATCH OUT, SHE'S ALWAYS <u>14_____</u> , SO
SHE SMELLS LIKE A/AN <u>15_____</u> <u>16_____</u> .

A SUDOKU PUZZLE ACTIVITY SHEET

A NUMBER PUZZLE THAT HAS ABSOLUTELY NOTHING
TO DO WITH NUMBERS—JUST THE WAY WE LIKE IT.

			8		9		2	3
	9	2	7	3			1	
8				2		4	7	
2				7			5	4
4	5	7	9			3		1
	1				6	7	8	
	7	5	2	4	8		9	
1	8	4	6	9		2	3	
6	2	9	5			8		7

HOW TO PLAY

JUST IN CASE YOU HAVE BEEN LOCKED AWAY IN A CULT FOR THE PAST TWENTY YEARS—SUDOKU IS
PLAYED ON A GRID OF 81 SPACES. WITHIN THIS ARE 9 'SQUARES' (EACH MADE OF A 3 BY 3 GRID).
EACH ROW, COLUMN, AND SQUARE MUST BE FILLED WITH THE NUMBERS 1-9, WITHOUT REPEATING
ANY NUMBERS WITHIN THE ROW, COLUMN, OR SQUARE. IT'S EASY—IN THEORY.

WHAT ARE THESE PEOPLE DOING?

A. STARTING A BAR FIGHT
B. WATER SKIING

A. DELIVERING AN UPPERCUT
B. GOING BOWLING

BONUS FUN!
DRAW IN THEIR
ACTIVITIES.

A. WRESTLING AN ALLIGATOR
B. PLAYING TENNIS

A. AVOIDING DOG POOP
B. PLAYING SOCCER

```
A D X M E B R A D L E Y C O O P E R
J X N X O C N O S S R D A B E K B U
C A D K Y M Q A R K K Y V V Y C U Y I
H G N V L A O N M U B V R A T I W Y
R J O E Z J V L K Y R U L V X J R M
I Q U K A A J F L E P B R W E E Z A
S H D D K N A S L Y N O Q F T R O R
T J R V A E E Y X A S M E L R B C G
O O W Y J H F G I X D H A H P E U U
P N Z W V M F L A I M W A R L D V E
H B O Z V V E R E R O U O N I E I R
E E Y F J A M T I H O H G D N N R I
R N E W H R N S S E Y F D X W O O T
M J R C O O E L T U D U A Z Y G N E
E A I T M T E A M O R L N L W U C M
L M A L T A C W G L Y I A Y O C I O
O I G F H L R K U P L G K N F X J R
N N B C P N L A P K T T X V D N J E
I H I W U N P U L G O H W J H E L A
U M E L I Z A B E T H B A N K S R U
```

FIND THESE CELEBRITIES

JANEANE GAROFALO
CHRISTOPHER MELONI
JUDAH FRIEDLANDER
MARGUERITE MOREAU
MICHAEL SHOWALTER

MOLLY SHANNON
ELIZABETH BANKS
BRADLEY COOPER
H JON BENJAMIN
MICHAEL IAN BLACK

PAUL RUDD
AMY POEHLER
KEN MARINO

BONUS:
WHAT DO
THEY ALL
HAVE IN
COMMON?

A MAKE-A-LIST ACTIVITY SHEET

ALL OF THE CELEBRITIES THAT I HONESTLY
SHOULD BE MORE FAMOUS THAN.

1 _____

2 _____

3 _____

4 _____

5 _____

6 _____

7 _____

8 _____

9 _____

10 _____

11 _____

12 _____

13 _____

14 _____

15 _____

16 _____

17 _____

18 _____

BONUS FUN:
WHY STOP AT 18?
FEEL FREE TO
USE SOME SCRAP
PAPER, TOO

103

CAN YOU SPOT THE DIFFERENCE?
ACTIVITY SHEET

HINT: IT'S A
TRICK QUESTION.
THEY'RE EXACTLY
THE SAME.

A MAKE-A-LIST ACTIVITY SHEET

A LIST OF THINGS THAT ROBOTS SHOULD BE
DOING NOW THAT IT'S THE 21ST CENTURY.

1 _____

2 _____

3 _____

4 _____

5 _____

6 _____

7 _____

8 _____

9 _____

10 _____

11 _____

12 _____

13 _____

14 _____

15 _____

16 _____

17 _____

18 _____

BONUS FUN:
WHY STOP AT 18?
FEEL FREE TO
USE SOME SCRAP
PAPER, TOO

CRACK THE CODE FOR AN IMPORTANT MESSAGE!

BONUS FUN:
DRAW IN A MOUSE
GIVING THIS BIRD
A HIGH FIVE.

A DOTS AND BOXES GAME SHEET

PSST: YOU'LL NEED A FRIEND (OR STRANGER) TO PLAY THIS ONE WITH—OTHERWISE YOU'LL DEFINITELY WIN.

HOW TO PLAY

TWO PLAYERS TAKE TURNS ADDING A SINGLE HORIZONTAL OR VERTICAL LINE BETWEEN 2 UNJOINED ADJACENT DOTS. A PLAYER WHO COMPLETES THE FOURTH SIDE OF A 1 BY 1 BOX EARNS ONE POINT AND TAKES ANOTHER TURN (PLACING THEIR INITIAL INSIDE THE BOX). WHEN NO MORE PLAYS CAN BE LEGALLY MADE, THE PLAYER WITH THE MOST POINTS IS DECLARED THE WINNER.

```
W C L T W S B L U E N O S E I P B V
V H Y S H Z J Y M Z O G C G Y S I Z
B I D D D E W D R O P P E R G A G M
E C A L B S C Q R V H X A Y S D C J
V A W B N T E A C F R Q E Y Y N H S
T G V P O R P O T S G N D G Q R E O
G O H I O U X K O S O A O N V O E C
F L W F D G E M Y L P V Z C T S S K
J I N J L G L A A G C A Y N Z A E D
U G E H E L T B D B K G J F F X O O
I H Q V J E G N U K N M O A V B L L
C T R J U B T M G P N C R T M R B L
E N E Q I U I C Y M I T T W W A O A
J I D J C G I G G L E W A T E R S G
O N I N E G O F A F H P R L S A Z E
I G P F K Y W B E A N S H O O T E R
N S K N O W Y O U R O N I O N S L G
T D N B G V I X X P U S B Q U V K L
C Y O N O C K P O D K Y N Y V E B P
H I J K Q R C E B U Z Z E R X X B J
```

FIND THESE WORDS

BALONEY
BLUENOSE
BUZZER
JUICE JOINT
ICY MITT

BEAN SHOOTER
GIGGLE WATER
DEWDROPPER
BIG CHEESE
SOCKDOLLAGER

CHICAGO LIGHTNING
KNOW YOUR ONIONS
THE CAT'S PAJAMAS
NOODLE JUICE
STRUGGLE BUGGY

IMPROVE THE NATIONAL MONUMENT (MOUNT RUSHMORE EDITION)

WE DIDN'T DRAW THIS, BUT WE GIVE OUR CONDOLENCES TO THE DESCENDANTS OF TEDDY ROOSEVELT.

PSST: PUT WHOEVER YOU WANT ON THERE. BONUS POINTS IF THEY AREN'T DEAD WHITE GUYS.

A FILL-IN-THE-BLANK STORY ACTIVITY SHEET

ANSWER THE QUESTIONS BELOW AND USE THEM TO COMPLETE THE STORY ON THE NEXT PAGE.

1. NAME A DECADE

2. NAME A BUSINESS OR RESTUARANT

3. NAME A VERB THAT ENDS IN 'ING'

4. NAME AN ADJECTIVE

5. NAME A PLURAL PLACE

6. NAME A PLURAL GROUP OF PEOPLE

7. NAME AN ACTION VERB

8. NAME AN OBJECT OR ANIMAL

9. NAME A DAY OF THE WEEK

10. NAME A PAST-TENSE VERB

11. NAME AN ADJECTIVE

12. NAME A NOUN

13. NAME AN ADJECTIVE

14. NAME AN ACTION VERB

ROSEMARIE

BONUS FUN:
DRAW IN THE CRIME
SCENE THAT SHE IS
FLEEING FROM

112

A HAUNTED DOLL COLORING SHEET (AND ORIGIN STORY)

> PSST: FLIP TO THE PREVIOUS PAGE AND FILL OUT THE QUESTIONS—NOW USE THEM TO COMPLETE THE STORY.

ROSEMARIE LEARNED TO RUN FAST GROWING UP IN THE __1__ NEXT TO THE WORLD'S FIRST __2__ . NOT A DAY WOULD GO BY THAT SHE WASN'T OUT __3__ THROUGH THE __4__ __5__ IN TOWN. THE LOCAL __6__ TRIED TO TELL HER THAT IT WAS DANGEROUS, BUT SHE TOLD THEM TO GO __7__ A/AN __8__ . ONE __9__ THOUGH, SHE __10__ HER LESSON WHEN SHE RAN PAST A/AN __11__ __12__ THAT PUT A SPELL ON HER AND TURNED HER INTO ONE OF THOSE __13__ DOLLS THAT CAN __14__ ITSELF.

A MAKE-A-LIST ACTIVITY SHEET

POPULAR THANKSGIVING SIDE DISHES,
RANKED FROM BEST TO WORST.

1 _____

2 _____

3 _____

4 _____

5 _____

6 _____

7 _____

8 _____

9 _____

10 _____

11 _____

12 _____

13 _____

14 _____

15 _____

16 _____

17 _____

18 _____

BONUS FUN:
WHY STOP AT 18?
FEEL FREE TO
USE SOME SCRAP
PAPER, TOO

A KINDA-SHADY-LOOKING FISH COLORING SHEET

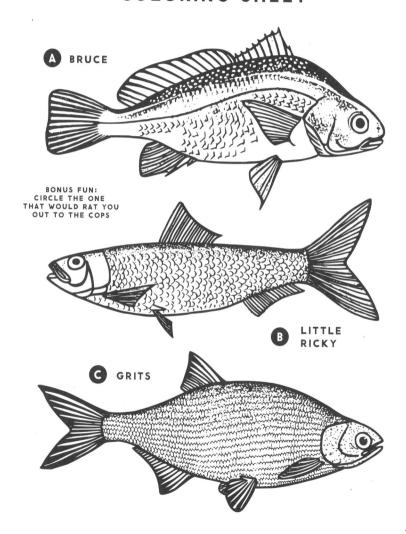

A BRUCE

BONUS FUN:
CIRCLE THE ONE
THAT WOULD RAT YOU
OUT TO THE COPS

B LITTLE RICKY

C GRITS

A SUDOKU PUZZLE ACTIVITY SHEET

A NUMBER PUZZLE THAT HAS ABSOLUTELY NOTHING
TO DO WITH NUMBERS—JUST THE WAY WE LIKE IT.

	3			4			1	
4	6	7		1	9	5		
1	8		7			3	4	6
		5	1		2	6	9	3
	9		4			7		2
6							8	1
2			9		1			
3		8	2		4	1	6	9
	1	4	6		8	2	7	5

HOW TO PLAY

JUST IN CASE YOU HAVE BEEN LOCKED AWAY IN A CULT FOR THE PAST TWENTY YEARS—SUDOKU IS
PLAYED ON A GRID OF 81 SPACES. WITHIN THIS ARE 9 'SQUARES' (EACH MADE OF A 3 BY 3 GRID).
EACH ROW, COLUMN, AND SQUARE MUST BE FILLED WITH THE NUMBERS 1-9, WITHOUT REPEATING
ANY NUMBERS WITHIN THE ROW, COLUMN, OR SQUARE. IT'S EASY—IN THEORY.

A MAKE-A-LIST ACTIVITY SHEET

IMPORTANT THINGS THAT I WAS WORRIED
ABOUT WHEN I WAS EIGHT YEARS OLD.

1 _____

2 _____

3 _____

4 _____

5 _____

6 _____

7 _____

8 _____

9 _____

10 _____

11 _____

12 _____

13 _____

14 _____

15 _____

16 _____

17 _____

18 _____

BONUS FUN:
WHY STOP AT 18?
FEEL FREE TO
USE SOME SCRAP
PAPER, TOO

A DOTS AND BOXES GAME SHEET

PSST: YOU'LL NEED A FRIEND (OR STRANGER) TO PLAY
THIS ONE WITH—OTHERWISE YOU'LL DEFINITELY WIN.

HOW TO PLAY

TWO PLAYERS TAKE TURNS ADDING A SINGLE HORIZONTAL OR VERTICAL LINE BETWEEN 2 UNJOINED
ADJACENT DOTS. A PLAYER WHO COMPLETES THE FOURTH SIDE OF A 1 BY 1 BOX EARNS ONE POINT
AND TAKES ANOTHER TURN (PLACING THEIR INITIAL INSIDE THE BOX). WHEN NO MORE PLAYS CAN BE
LEGALLY MADE, THE PLAYER WITH THE MOST POINTS IS DECLARED THE WINNER.

CRACK THE CODE FOR AN IMPORTANT MESSAGE!

BONUS FUN:
IDENTIFY THAT
WEIRD LOOKING
OBJECT ABOVE.

WHAT ARE THESE PEOPLE DOING?

A. BILL MAHER HULA HOOPING
B. CROSS-COUNTRY SKIING

A. GREEN SCREEN ACTING
B. SPEED SKATING

**BONUS FUN!
DRAW IN THEIR
ACTIVITIES.**

A. WATCHING A VASE SHATTER
B. PLAYING BASKETBALL

A. LOOKING FOR A CONTACT
B. PLAYING GOLF

A STATE MOTTO ACTIVITY SHEET

WRITE YOUR OWN (MORE ACCURATE) STATE
MOTTO AT THE BOTTOM OF EACH PLATE.

BUCKEYE STATE

OHIO

SIOUX STATE

N. DAKOTA

PEACH STATE

GEORGIA

EMPIRE STATE

NEW YORK

WHEAT STATE

KANSAS

SUNSHINE STATE

FLORIDA

LONE STAR STATE

TEXAS

SILVER STATE

NEVADA

COMPLETE THE DRAWING
TO HELP THIS DINOSAUR'S
DREAM COME TRUE.

SOMEDAY, I WANT TO
BE A SHOE MODEL.

```
S F G R A N D A D D Y P U R P L E O
N U B T M D X Z N D U B W A F A J R
M O P L D L U T M N M P J B T C L E
B W R E C Z I V I Z G N E W W O M L
Z L U T R Z K E E H F V V M W N Y T
X U U F H S G Q Q J E K X O U F I G
S M Z E L E I K Q U J W D H Q I H O
O K E R D A R L U O E I U H U D S L
U Y E Q P R X N V K W O U O J E L D
R M N R C N E K L E J Q N W U N K E
D I Q E O E F A T I R W D S M T H N
I Z R U U F D I M J G H A B E I J G
E P T E H U H K Y A T H A K N A C O
S N H M E W U E P X E Y T Z J L J A
E I I D V M E N Z V N O N S E S C T
L D P I N E A P P L E E X P R E S S
H M R B P D K I M A U I W O W I E B
L V F R U I T Y P E B B L E S N U N
T X O P J C Y H A O P J L Y L V O Q
S A C A P U L C O G O L D K Q W Z K
```

FIND THESE PHRASES

ACAPULCO GOLD
GOLDEN GOAT
FRUITY PEBBLES
LA CONFIDENTIAL

GRANDADDY PURPLE
NORTHERN LIGHTS
SUPER SILVER HAZE
PINEAPPLE EXPRESS

BLUE DREAM
WHITE WIDOW
MAUI WOWIE
SOUR DIESEL

BONUS:
WHAT DO THEY ALL HAVE IN COMMON?

A FILL-IN-THE-BLANK STORY ACTIVITY SHEET

ANSWER THE QUESTIONS BELOW AND USE THEM TO COMPLETE THE STORY ON THE NEXT PAGE.

1. NAME A FOOD

2. NAME A DECADE

3. NAME AN ADJECTIVE

4. NAME AN ACTIVITY

5. NAME A PAST-TENSE VERB

6. NAME AN ADJECTIVE

7. NAME AN ANIMAL OR PERSON

8. NAME A PAST-TENSE ACTIVITY

9. NAME AN ADJECTIVE

10. NAME A YEAR

11. NAME A PLURAL APPLIANCE

12. NAME AN ADJECTIVE

13. NAME A PLURAL ITEM OF CLOTHING

14. NAME A PLACE

PRUDENCE

BONUS FUN:
DRAW IN THE GHOST
FRIEND THAT SHE'S
WAVING TO

A HAUNTED DOLL COLORING SHEET (AND ORIGIN STORY)

PSST: FLIP TO THE PREVIOUS PAGE AND FILL OUT THE QUESTIONS—NOW USE THEM TO COMPLETE THE STORY.

LIFE AS A/AN ¹_____ FARMER IN THE ²_____ WAS ³_____ WORK. THAT'S WHY PRUDENCE DECIDED TO TAKE A BREAK AND ⁴_____ IN THE MIDDLE OF THE FIELD. TRAGICALLY, SHE WAS ⁵_____ BY A/AN ⁶_____ ⁷_____ WHILE SHE ⁸_____ . LUCKILY SHE WAS REINCARNATED, BUT IT'S JUST TOO BAD THAT IT WAS INSIDE OF A ⁹_____ , LIFELESS DOLL IN ¹⁰_____ . THE MODERN WORLD SCARES HER, ESPECIALLY ¹¹_____ AND ¹²_____ ¹³_____ . WHICH IS UNFORTUNATE, SINCE SHE'S STUCK INSIDE OF A/AN ¹⁴_____ .

A SUDOKU PUZZLE ACTIVITY SHEET

A NUMBER PUZZLE THAT HAS ABSOLUTELY NOTHING
TO DO WITH NUMBERS—JUST THE WAY WE LIKE IT.

4	8	7			1			
3				8				7
5	6		3				2	
6		3	9			7		2
2		5		1	3	9	8	4
9		8	7	5	2			
8	5			1		7	2	9	6
	2			6				
1	3		2	9	4			

HOW TO PLAY

JUST IN CASE YOU HAVE BEEN LOCKED AWAY IN A CULT FOR THE PAST TWENTY YEARS—SUDOKU IS
PLAYED ON A GRID OF 81 SPACES. WITHIN THIS ARE 9 'SQUARES' (EACH MADE OF A 3 BY 3 GRID).
EACH ROW, COLUMN, AND SQUARE MUST BE FILLED WITH THE NUMBERS 1-9, WITHOUT REPEATING
ANY NUMBERS WITHIN THE ROW, COLUMN, OR SQUARE. IT'S EASY—IN THEORY.

A MAKE-A-LIST ACTIVITY SHEET

CLEVER THINGS THAT I SHOULD HAVE
SAID DURING PAST ARGUEMENTS.

1 _____

2 _____

3 _____

4 _____

5 _____

6 _____

7 _____

8 _____

9 _____

10 _____

11 _____

12 _____

13 _____

14 _____

15 _____

16 _____

17 _____

18 _____

BONUS FUN:
WHY STOP AT 18?
FEEL FREE TO
USE SOME SCRAP
PAPER, TOO

START

FINISH

A HOMEOWNER'S ACTIVITY SHEET

CIRCLE EVERYTHING THAT THE LOCAL HOA
WILL THREATEN TO FINE YOU FOR.

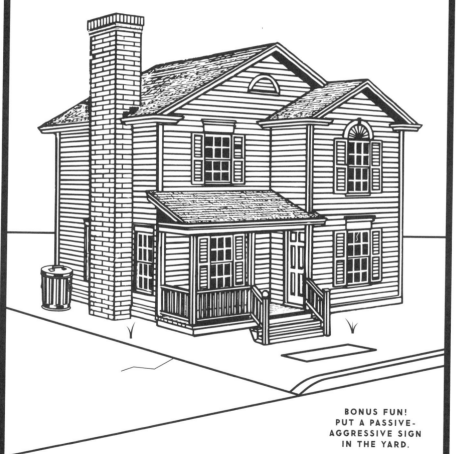

BONUS FUN!
PUT A PASSIVE-
AGGRESSIVE SIGN
IN THE YARD.

A MIDLIFE CRISIS COLORING SHEET

BONUS FUN!
GUESS EACH BOAT'S
RESALE VALUE

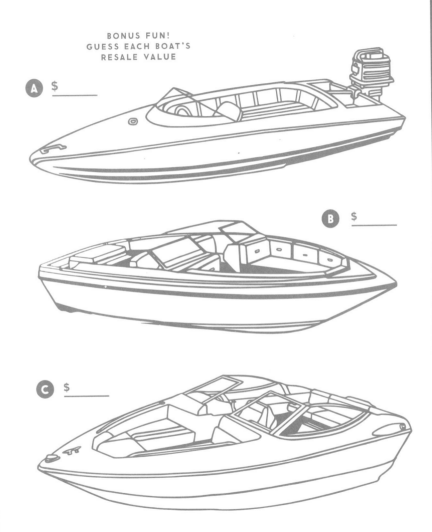

A $ _____

B $ _____

C $ _____

A DOTS AND BOXES GAME SHEET

PSST: YOU'LL NEED A FRIEND (OR STRANGER) TO PLAY THIS ONE WITH—OTHERWISE YOU'LL DEFINITELY WIN.

HOW TO PLAY

TWO PLAYERS TAKE TURNS ADDING A SINGLE HORIZONTAL OR VERTICAL LINE BETWEEN 2 UNJOINED ADJACENT DOTS. A PLAYER WHO COMPLETES THE FOURTH SIDE OF A 1 BY 1 BOX EARNS ONE POINT AND TAKES ANOTHER TURN (PLACING THEIR INITIAL INSIDE THE BOX). WHEN NO MORE PLAYS CAN BE LEGALLY MADE, THE PLAYER WITH THE MOST POINTS IS DECLARED THE WINNER.

133

COMPLETE THE DRAWING
TO HELP THIS DINOSAUR'S
DREAM COME TRUE

A CROSS-COUNTRY ROAD TRIP COLORING SHEET

YOU'LL NEVER ESCAPE THESE CARS ON THE ROAD. WHAT WILL THEIR CRUISE CONTROLS INEVIABLY BE SET TO?

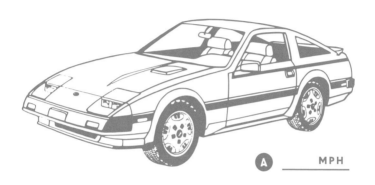

A _____ MPH

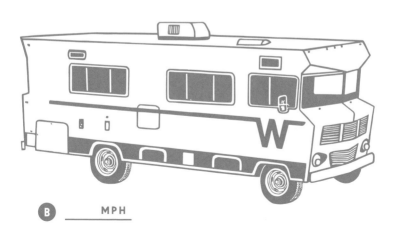

B _____ MPH

A MAKE-A-LIST ACTIVITY SHEET

A RUNNING LIST OF MADE UP PHRASES
THAT SOUND LIKE YOGA POSITIONS.

1 _____

2 _____

3 _____

4 _____

5 _____

6 _____

7 _____

8 _____

9 _____

10 _____

11 _____

12 _____

13 _____

14 _____

15 _____

16 _____

17 _____

18 _____

BONUS FUN:
WHY STOP AT 18?
FEEL FREE TO
USE SOME SCRAP
PAPER, TOO

A SUDOKU PUZZLE ACTIVITY SHEET

A NUMBER PUZZLE THAT HAS ABSOLUTELY NOTHING
TO DO WITH NUMBERS—JUST THE WAY WE LIKE IT.

8				4				
2		6	5			8		
7								
6	2		7	5	4			
5	3			1	9			
		4		6			2	5
		2				5	8	9
		5	6			4		3
	8			9		6	1	2

HOW TO PLAY

JUST IN CASE YOU HAVE BEEN LOCKED AWAY IN A CULT FOR THE PAST TWENTY YEARS—SUDOKU IS
PLAYED ON A GRID OF 81 SPACES. WITHIN THIS ARE 9 'SQUARES' (EACH MADE OF A 3 BY 3 GRID).
EACH ROW, COLUMN, AND SQUARE MUST BE FILLED WITH THE NUMBERS 1-9, WITHOUT REPEATING
ANY NUMBERS WITHIN THE ROW, COLUMN, OR SQUARE. IT'S EASY—IN THEORY.

PICK THE TOTALLY REASONABLE RESPONSE FOR EACH BUG

A. CRY AND HOPE FOR THE BEST
B. THROW A SHOE AT IT

A. WELCOME YOUR NEW ROOMIE
B. SCREAM AND RUN AWAY

A. GOOGLE IT AND PRAY
B. SMASH IT WITH PHONE BOOK

A. CALL YOUR MOM
B. STAND ON A CHAIR & YELL

A. CALL YOUR REALTOR
B. JUST BURN THE HOUSE DOWN

A. TRY TO CATCH & RELEASE IT
B. FLAIL WILDLY AT IT

A FILL-IN-THE-BLANK STORY ACTIVITY SHEET

ANSWER THE QUESTIONS BELOW AND USE THEM TO COMPLETE THE STORY ON THE NEXT PAGE.

1. NAME AN OCCUPATION

2. NAME A DECADE

3. NAME AN ADJECTIVE

4. NAME A BODY PART

5. NAME A PAST-TENSE VERB

6. NAME AN ADJECTIVE

7. NAME AN ANIMAL OR PERSON

8. NAME A PAST-TENSE VERB

9. NAME AN ADJECTIVE

10. NAME A LENGTH OF TIME

11. NAME A THIRD-PERSON ACTION VERB

12. NAME A PLURAL NOUN

13. NAME A NOUN

14. NAME AN ACTION VERB

15. NAME A THIRD-PERSON ACTION VERB

16. NAME AN ANIMAL OR PERSON

MADELINE

BONUS FUN:
DON'T FORGET TO
DRAW IN ALL OF THE
SOULS THAT SHE
HAS CAPTURED OVER
THE YEARS

A HAUNTED DOLL COLORING SHEET (AND ORIGIN STORY)

PSST: FLIP TO THE PREVIOUS PAGE AND FILL OUT THE QUESTIONS—NOW USE THEM TO COMPLETE THE STORY.

IT WAS HARD BEING A/AN <u>1   </u> IN THE EARLY <u>2   </u>. THANKS TO HER <u>3   </u> <u>4   </u> , MADELINE WAS TRAGICALLY <u>5   </u> BY A/AN <u>6   </u> <u>7   </u>. HER SOUL WAS SUDDENLY <u>8   </u> INTO A/AN <u>9   </u> DOLL, TRAPPING IT FOR <u>10   </u> UNLESS SHE <u>11   </u> ENOUGH <u>12   </u>. DON'T WORRY, SHE ONLY COMES TO LIFE IF THE <u>13   </u> STARTS TO <u>14   </u>. OTHERWISE, SHE JUST APPEARS WHILE YOU SLEEP AND LOUDLY <u>15   </u> FOR HER MISSING <u>16   </u>. LIKE, A LOT. YOU'LL GET USED TO IT.

DECLINING UNKNOWN CALLERS
COLORING SHEET

A SUDOKU PUZZLE ACTIVITY SHEET

A NUMBER PUZZLE THAT HAS ABSOLUTELY NOTHING
TO DO WITH NUMBERS—JUST THE WAY WE LIKE IT.

	5	1	7				3	
	2				1	5		8
	3		2		5		4	
9				3	4		1	6
	7	6						
		3	6			2	8	
2					3		6	4
	1			2		3		5
		4	1	5		8	2	

HOW TO PLAY

JUST IN CASE YOU HAVE BEEN LOCKED AWAY IN A CULT FOR THE PAST TWENTY YEARS—SUDOKU IS
PLAYED ON A GRID OF 81 SPACES. WITHIN THIS ARE 9 'SQUARES' (EACH MADE OF A 3 BY 3 GRID).
EACH ROW, COLUMN, AND SQUARE MUST BE FILLED WITH THE NUMBERS 1-9, WITHOUT REPEATING
ANY NUMBERS WITHIN THE ROW, COLUMN, OR SQUARE. IT'S EASY—IN THEORY.

A DOTS AND BOXES GAME SHEET

PSST: YOU'LL NEED A FRIEND (OR STRANGER) TO PLAY THIS ONE WITH—OTHERWISE YOU'LL DEFINITELY WIN.

HOW TO PLAY

TWO PLAYERS TAKE TURNS ADDING A SINGLE HORIZONTAL OR VERTICAL LINE BETWEEN 2 UNJOINED ADJACENT DOTS. A PLAYER WHO COMPLETES THE FOURTH SIDE OF A 1 BY 1 BOX EARNS ONE POINT AND TAKES ANOTHER TURN (PLACING THEIR INITIAL INSIDE THE BOX). WHEN NO MORE PLAYS CAN BE LEGALLY MADE, THE PLAYER WITH THE MOST POINTS IS DECLARED THE WINNER.

```
Q K U K V D P M N A G B X Q W W Y Z
I F F P P I S A D R O R O H U T O K
B K Y C H C P V R B O V O S U Q G Y
A M H A T P H E A W S S I O L D O T
W E I O J L P R R Y E K Y O S B E Z
F R T V L P M I P X S J B J N T Q C
N L F J I L I C A Q E L K A L E E C
A I G H N L Y K J R F D F R S C C R
F N C A B B R W O Q Y M P D Z W V V
I J E S T E R X O D C M V N V O V M
C H U E D H B W K O F K I G R L U B
P X A L U U Y B N V D C F C J F T W
U H C P A Y B A C K X I G O X M E O
Y G O O N N M D H Z Y Y P S A A U V
I J X E Y G U W X H I M D Q P N S S
J C L H N P W W Q E X D M G V Q V L
R W E A X I T J Z C W L E D N P C I
U S H M P W X E X H T P V G G L L D
N O A L A Z H C H A R L I E Q O I E
L R S T I N G E R M Z A C O U G A R
```

FIND THESE WORDS

BONUS:
WHAT DO
THEY ALL
HAVE IN
COMMON?

PHOENIX
STINGER
SLIDER
WOLFMAN

BOB
COUGAR
GOOSE
MERLIN

CHARLIE
HANDMAN
JESTER
PAYBACK
VIPER

MAVERICK
CHIPPER
HOLLYWOOD
ROOSTER
FANBOY

START

FINISH

ARE THEY CAPABLE OF MURDER?

BONUS FUN! CIRCLE THE ONES THAT WOULD EAT YOUR BODY

YES / NO

YES / NO

YES / NO

YES / NO

YES / NO

YES / NO

IDENTIFY THE LEAST HUMANE FORM OF TORTURE ACTIVITY SHEET

BONUS: WRITE IN HOW MUCH EACH OF THESE ITEMS WOULD COST ON CRAIGSLIST.

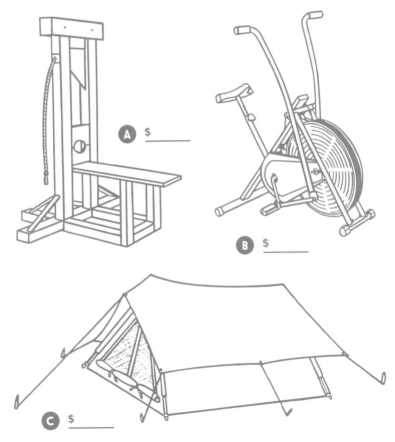

A $ _____

B $ _____

C $ _____

A DOTS AND BOXES GAME SHEET

PSST: YOU'LL NEED A FRIEND (OR STRANGER) TO PLAY
THIS ONE WITH—OTHERWISE YOU'LL DEFINITELY WIN.

HOW TO PLAY

TWO PLAYERS TAKE TURNS ADDING A SINGLE HORIZONTAL OR VERTICAL LINE BETWEEN 2 UNJOINED
ADJACENT DOTS. A PLAYER WHO COMPLETES THE FOURTH SIDE OF A 1 BY 1 BOX EARNS ONE POINT
AND TAKES ANOTHER TURN (PLACING THEIR INITIAL INSIDE THE BOX). WHEN NO MORE PLAYS CAN BE
LEGALLY MADE, THE PLAYER WITH THE MOST POINTS IS DECLARED THE WINNER.

A MAKE-A-LIST ACTIVITY SHEET

A LIST OF MOVIE TITLES THAT ALSO
HAPPEN TO DESCRIBE MY SEX LIFE.

1 _____

2 _____

3 _____

4 _____

5 _____

6 _____

7 _____

8 _____

9 _____

10 _____

11 _____

12 _____

13 _____

14 _____

15 _____

16 _____

17 _____

18 _____

BONUS FUN:
WHY STOP AT 18?
FEEL FREE TO
USE SOME SCRAP
PAPER, TOO

CRACK THE CODE FOR AN IMPORTANT MESSAGE!

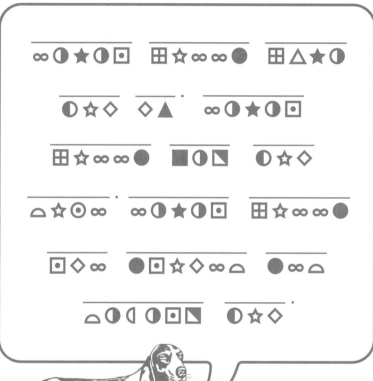

BONUS FUN!
DRAW IN WHAT
HE IS LIKELY
PEEING ON

A RUNNING-AWAY-FROM-LIFE ACTIVITY SHEET

DRAW YOUR
SELF-PORTRAIT
ON THE SIDE OF
THE CARTON.

BONUS FUN!
WHAT ARE YOU
ESCAPING?

A FILL-IN-THE-BLANK STORY ACTIVITY SHEET

ANSWER THE QUESTIONS BELOW AND USE THEM TO COMPLETE THE STORY ON THE NEXT PAGE.

1. NAME A PLURAL NOUN

2. NAME AN ACTION VERB

3. NAME AN EMOTION

4. NAME AN ANIMAL OR OBJECT

5. NAME AN ADJECTIVE

6. NAME A LOCATION

7. NAME A CITY

8. NAME AN ADJECTIVE

9. NAME AN OBJECT OR FOOD

10. NAME AN OBJECT

11. NAME AN ADVERB

12. NAME AN ADJECTIVE

13. NAME A LENGTH OF TIME

14. NAME A PLURAL NOUN

HENRIETTA

BONUS FUN:
DRAW WHAT SHE'S
PAINTING—YOUR
UNTIMELY DEATH

A HAUNTED DOLL COLORING SHEET (AND ORIGIN STORY)

PSST: FLIP TO THE PREVIOUS PAGE AND FILL OUT THE QUESTIONS—NOW USE THEM TO COMPLETE THE STORY.

ALL OF THE <u>1</u>_____ WARNED HER ABOUT GOING TO ART SCHOOL, BUT HENRIETTA WOULDN'T <u>2</u>_____. SHE WAS SO <u>3</u>_____ ON HER FIRST DAY, WHEN THE CLASS WAS TO MEET FOR A/AN <u>4</u>_____ DRAWING CLASS AT THE <u>5</u>_____ <u>6</u>_____ NEAR THE EDGE OF <u>7</u>_____. EVERYTHING WAS GOING GREAT UNTIL HENRIETTA ATE A <u>8</u>_____ <u>9</u>_____ THAT SHE FOUND ON THE <u>10</u>_____. THE TOXINS INSIDE <u>11</u>_____ TRANSFORMED HER INTO A <u>12</u>_____ DOLL IN A MATTER OF <u>13</u>_____, FOREVER DOOMED TO PAINT <u>14</u>_____ FOR ETERNITY.

A MAKE-A-LIST ACTIVITY SHEET

IF MY LIFE HAD A SOUNDTRACK, THESE
SONGS WOULD HAVE TO BE ON IT.

1 _____

2 _____

3 _____

4 _____

5 _____

6 _____

7 _____

8 _____

9 _____

10 _____

11 _____

12 _____

13 _____

14 _____

15 _____

16 _____

17 _____

18 _____

BONUS FUN:
WHY STOP AT 18?
FEEL FREE TO
USE SOME SCRAP
PAPER, TOO

WHAT ARE THESE BIRDS THINKING?

ADD IN THEIR INNER DIALOGUE WHILE THEY'RE UP THERE IN THE TREES—SILENTLY JUDGING YOU.

START

FINISH

A SUDOKU PUZZLE ACTIVITY SHEET

A NUMBER PUZZLE THAT HAS ABSOLUTELY NOTHING TO DO WITH NUMBERS—JUST THE WAY WE LIKE IT.

		5					1	3
	8		5					
			1	2				
	1							
		4	7	5	9			
8	6			2	3	9	4	5
			3			8		
6		1		7		2	3	
	4		2		1	5	9	7

HOW TO PLAY

JUST IN CASE YOU HAVE BEEN LOCKED AWAY IN A CULT FOR THE PAST TWENTY YEARS—SUDOKU IS PLAYED ON A GRID OF 81 SPACES. WITHIN THIS ARE 9 'SQUARES' (EACH MADE OF A 3 BY 3 GRID). EACH ROW, COLUMN, AND SQUARE MUST BE FILLED WITH THE NUMBERS 1-9, WITHOUT REPEATING ANY NUMBERS WITHIN THE ROW, COLUMN, OR SQUARE. IT'S EASY—IN THEORY.

A SUDOKU PUZZLE ACTIVITY SHEET

A NUMBER PUZZLE THAT HAS ABSOLUTELY NOTHING TO DO WITH NUMBERS—JUST THE WAY WE LIKE IT.

1		2			3	7	4	
9	6		4	7	2			3
	3	1		8	5	2		
4		9	7					
	1	6				2		5
	5		3		6			
2		8	6	5	4			
6	9	1					5	
5		4		8	1		3	

HOW TO PLAY

JUST IN CASE YOU HAVE BEEN LOCKED AWAY IN A CULT FOR THE PAST TWENTY YEARS—SUDOKU IS PLAYED ON A GRID OF 81 SPACES. WITHIN THIS ARE 9 'SQUARES' (EACH MADE OF A 3 BY 3 GRID). EACH ROW, COLUMN, AND SQUARE MUST BE FILLED WITH THE NUMBERS 1-9, WITHOUT REPEATING ANY NUMBERS WITHIN THE ROW, COLUMN, OR SQUARE. IT'S EASY—IN THEORY.

NAME THE UNCONVENTIAL HOUSE PETS ACTIVITY SHEET

WHICH NAME IS MOST BEFITTING OF THESE DISTINGUISHED COMPANIONS?

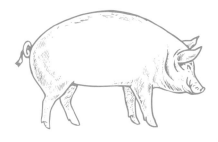

A. BREAKFAST FOR DINNER
B. DEBRA

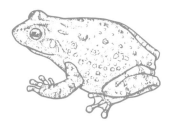

A. MR. WELLINGTON
B. FROGGY FROG FROG

A. SQUIGGLES
B. THE GRAVE DIGGER

A. COLONEL STICKY
B. SHELL BIV DEVO

```
A R A I N B O W B R I T E A Z G S P
Z C T S C O C O A H O O T S L W D M
N U Z A O P Q H M A G I C P U F F S
C D C A O H M C R A Z Y C O W P Y Y
S U E H I D D E N T R E A S U R E S
W P J E W A F F E L O S B I Q S W G
M K R C P W Y U M M Y M U M M Y J W
E M S I R S E Y G O M H F X Q E O D
Z N N R N Y E S C E O U B D D L U F
N C H C Q K P A A P M N I A L C J G
M H H U I S L V C Z A N S E Z K Z S
L O E S K J T E Z R F J F T R J V Y
I C J F Y E F R S A U E C V O H B H
G O J U A N C Y B P P N M B E N I P
C D F N I O B X N A A Z C J F V E I
D O F C L O E M R O J N Y H K A B S
H N P M E X P G Q C V E G I L J R Y
S U G A R K R I N K L E S L M J R K
T T M E V I P W S M N M O E E H A H
C S F C S Z J P Z Z H N Z N I S A I
```

FIND THESE PHRASES

BONUS:
WHAT DO THEY ALL HAVE IN COMMON?

CRAZY COW
MAGIC PUFFS
WAFFLEOS

CHOCO DONUTS
MOONSTONES
YUMMY MUMMY
RAINBOW BRITE
COCOA HOOTS

SPRINKLE SPANGLES
HIDDEN TREASURES
SUGAR KRINKLES
CIRCUS FUN
DEEP SEA CRUNCH

```
D C T Q O O P S X Z V E P E A I X F
G R X B P O W E R F U L M U S K O X
Q Y K B A A U N I C O R N N U R S E
B I B E L S K L T I X O V J P S R O
M U Q A E A P P R A S B C B E Q U R
U F M U S S E S I U P B A L R P L U
S L A T C S O C C K A I R L F E E D
Q A L I E Y B J K E C G R Q E B B E
T N W F N M X P Y E E I Q V C Y R B
Z D P U T A K R M K U S U G T I E B
E M R L T N Z S I X N U O Z S I A N
K E K S R N N G N S I N E G U E K Z
Q R A P E E Q N X Y C G W M N J I L
P M U I E Q Q V B S O O Q Q F A N I
Y A K N S U I E M Y R D Z H L L G D
D I O S H I U V T R N D F E O P M Q
C D E T A N T J G U L E A D W A O R
T C A E R S R X V V M S Y W E L T N
O C L R K N A I B P B S T W R D H X
Y J O Z D D S A J Y P W Q K Q T Y J
```

FIND THESE PHRASES

BEAUTIFUL SPINSTER
LAND MERMAID
PERFECT SUNFLOWER
SASSY MANNEQUIN
SUN GODDESS
UNICORN NURSE

OPALESCENT TREE SHARK
POWERFUL MUSK OX
RULE-BREAKING MOTH
SPACE UNICORN
TRICKY MINX

BONUS:
WHAT DO THEY ALL HAVE IN COMMON?

A MAKE-A-LIST ACTIVITY SHEET

A RUNNING LIST OF MY FAVORITE JAMS
(ALTERNATING SONGS & PRESERVES)

1 _____

2 _____

3 _____

4 _____

5 _____

6 _____

7 _____

8 _____

9 _____

10 _____

11 _____

12 _____

13 _____

14 _____

15 _____

16 _____

17 _____

18 _____

BONUS FUN:
WHY STOP AT 18?
FEEL FREE TO
USE SOME SCRAP
PAPER, TOO

WHAT IS THIS BIRD MAD ABOUT?

THESE 2 SPARROWS CLEARLY DID SOMETHING WRONG.
ADD IN THE THOUGHTS OF THE BIRD THEY OFFENDED.

A FILL-IN-THE-BLANK STORY ACTIVITY SHEET

ANSWER THE QUESTIONS BELOW AND USE THEM TO COMPLETE THE STORY ON THE NEXT PAGE.

1. NAME AN ADJECTIVE ENDING IN 'EST'

2. NAME AN ACTIVITY

3. NAME A PLACE

4. NAME AN ADJECTIVE

5. NAME AN ANIMAL OR PERSON

6. NAME A PLURAL BODY PART

7. NAME AN ACTION VERB

8. NAME AN ADJECTIVE

9. NAME AN PLURAL OBJECT OR ANIMAL

10. NAME AN ACTIVITY

11. NAME A PAST-TENSE VERB

12. NAME AN ADJECTIVE

13. NAME AN ACTION VERB

14. NAME A LENGTH OF TIME

15. NAME A NOUN

16. NAME A BODY PART

BERNADETTE

BONUS FUN:
DRAW IN THE
HOUSE SHE IS
HAUNTING

A HAUNTED DOLL COLORING SHEET (AND ORIGIN STORY)

PSST: FLIP TO THE PREVIOUS PAGE AND FILL OUT THE QUESTIONS—NOW USE THEM TO COMPLETE THE STORY.

BERNADETTE WAS THE ___1___
CHILD IN HER ___2___ CLASS IN
___3___ . ALL OF THE OTHER KIDS
WOULD TEASE HER, CALLING HER
NAMES LIKE ___4___ ___5___
___6___ AND ___7___ HER
___8___ ___9___ WHEN SHE WASN'T
LOOKING. ONE DAY AFTER ___10___
SHE WENT HOME AND ___11___ .
SUDDENLY, SHE WOKE UP AS A/AN
___12___ DOLL WITH THE ABILITY TO
___13___ . SHE WAS THRILLED, AND
SPENT THE NEXT ___14___ HAUNTING
HER CLASSMATES BY WHISPERING
' ___15___ ' INTO THEIR ___16___ .

GUESS-THE-NUMBER CASINO GAME

PLACE BETS ON WHAT NUMBER THE WHEEL
PICTURED BELOW WILL LAND ON.

IT'S 23. YOU
DO REALIZE THIS IS
PRINTED, RIGHT?

USELESS WAYS TO TRAVEL COLORING SHEET

BE SURE TO ESTIMATE HOW LONG YOUR
DAILY COMMUTE WOULD TAKE.

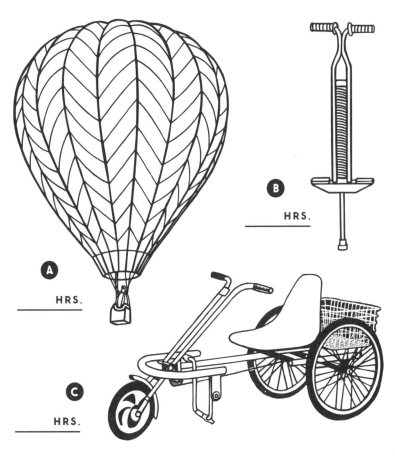

A _____ HRS.

B _____ HRS.

C _____ HRS.

A MAKE-A-LIST ACTIVITY SHEET

A RUNNING LIST OF THE WORST GIFTS
THAT I'VE EVER RECEIVED.

1 _____

2 _____

3 _____

4 _____

5 _____

6 _____

7 _____

8 _____

9 _____

10 _____

11 _____

12 _____

13 _____

14 _____

15 _____

16 _____

17 _____

18 _____

BONUS FUN:
WHY STOP AT 18?
FEEL FREE TO
USE SOME SCRAP
PAPER, TOO

A THIRD DATE COLORING SHEET

YOU GO BACK TO THEIR PLACE AFTERWARDS & SEE THIS.
DRAW WHAT THE REST OF THE ROOM LOOKS LIKE.

BONUS FUN:
ADD IN A BUNCH
OF CREEPY DOLLS
WATCHING YOU

A DOTS AND BOXES GAME SHEET

PSST: YOU'LL NEED A FRIEND (OR STRANGER) TO PLAY THIS ONE WITH—OTHERWISE YOU'LL DEFINITELY WIN.

HOW TO PLAY

TWO PLAYERS TAKE TURNS ADDING A SINGLE HORIZONTAL OR VERTICAL LINE BETWEEN 2 UNJOINED ADJACENT DOTS. A PLAYER WHO COMPLETES THE FOURTH SIDE OF A 1 BY 1 BOX EARNS ONE POINT AND TAKES ANOTHER TURN (PLACING THEIR INITIAL INSIDE THE BOX). WHEN NO MORE PLAYS CAN BE LEGALLY MADE, THE PLAYER WITH THE MOST POINTS IS DECLARED THE WINNER.

LOOKING FOR SOME ANSWERS?

IF IT'S ABOUT LIFE, YOU'RE ON YOUR OWN—BUT CHECK OUT THE NEXT FEW PAGES FOR HELP ON THE PUZZLES.

BONUS FUN:
DRAW THE GUY
WITH ALL OF THE
WRONG ANSWERS
BEHIND HIM.

RIGHT ANSWERS

```
F Y M R P F O S S T A C S X T L I F
A O T H A C S L O R G P R S C Y V A
N S O S H O W G I R L S Q J A O X J
T T B R R P C K N A M O W T A C Y A
A R V S P X C O C K T A I L T M T C
S I T H E E M O J I M O V I E S X K
T P H D I R T Y L O V E O U G A E A
I T E B A B B U W D G D M L B V L N
C E P O H W R R L R T E P T J I I D
F A O L U C E G H O S T S C A N S J
O S S E R N A I W L S I L G I G Z I
U E T R P K K T K N D B W T N C A L
R B M O S S I L S R T V A B E H I L
T G A S L U N I M F N G X R X R C N
V D N U R U G E V O L E H T J I B H
N S S T B W D N A F F W L O H S A L
M I J R D B A D L U V X C S E T N K
T R W I L D W I L D W E S T O M L A
X L V B J D N A S C V J D A Q A E X
I V H I Q V S W E P T A W A Y S B O
```

NOTES:

. . . .

. . . .

. . . .

. . . .

. . . .

. . . .

. . . .

BONUS: ALL GOLDEN
RASPBERRY AWARD WINNING
MOVIES

NOTES:

. . . .

. . . .

. . . .

. . . .

. . . .

. . . .

. . . .

. . . .

. . . .

. . . .

START

FINISH

NOTES:

3	5	1	7	6	9	4	2	8
4	7	2	3	8	1	5	6	9
8	6	9	2	5	4	1	3	7
5	1	6	9	4	2	7	8	3
7	4	8	1	3	6	9	5	2
9	2	3	5	7	8	6	1	4
1	9	4	8	2	5	3	7	6
6	8	7	4	1	3	2	9	5
2	3	5	6	9	7	8	4	1

```
S U L E Z E X H Y Z P F Q X B U O N
F P H R X W H Y N O T R S B E T Z O
U G E P V B P G E S U C P C V T A B
U N C E R T A I N B X O P M R Q K B
T S C D D A T N O U Z C O J A K K Q
Q L H D I F F K G A Y A L U M M J O
S Q F U N N C N M S T J T G D G V L
A R N Y P H O U W I N N E B A G O M
B B A N H X M S V E E N M D Q O Q I
S K L V I O X Z A C N G Q E J B P D
O X X M G B D I A U S P T V O L S S
N B Y L Z E G L K H R E Z C G O W L
Q Z T X W L P B L C R O D Q Q N O R
I F L O J D A H Z C O B G C V G E P
J F R T L U I U N I V W O N B N R J
H J Y I G P E O N A T X A P J Z B S
X X J W E U C T P D A T Z R J S U A
R Q R P X S H U R T H X V O D W P K
N Z M E M R B B K V H O O K E R K J
C N D F A C A P I N K M E V L X Z S
```

NOTES:

BONUS: ALL NAMES
OF TOWNS IN THE UNITED
STATES

NOTES:

WE'VE   BEEN

TRYING

TO   REACH   YOU

ABOUT   YOUR

CAR'S   EXTENDED

WARRANTY

NOTES:

BONUS: ACTORS THAT
WERE ONCE CONSIDERED TO
PLAY JAMES BOND

```
C G B A Q D Q O S E A N B E A N C V
X P S A D A M W E S T I K R D X O J
D O M I N I C W E S T E J N T Z A A
G R E X H A R R I S O N E T T R V M
M T V U A R A L P H F I E N N E S E
H C A B X R U W B B R Q C B G V R S
C L A C G T Y W J F V X H I F G I M
S I J O S U E G T G T Z R L L M C A
A N W G P B Z R D U C S I V G I H S
M T E J G S E A O S D N S R C C A O
N E G W F P A Y M L O T T F N H R N
E A N B U D U B O L A X I Q K A D C
I S J R W M W N A B J W A R A E B A
L T K M W L Y I M L K V N B B L U R
L W Q O V E D V Q T V M B Y N C R Y
N O B O R L L E A N I W A A L A T G
K O V T A D T Q C S F R L P B I O R
K D R B W F C H E Z E Z E E Q N N A
X U V E P J L H L P H T N N Z E F N
B Y P L I A M N E E S O N L Q W Y T
```

NOTES:
. . . .
. . . .
. . . .
. . . .
. . . .
. . . .
. . . .
. . . .

3	5	9	2	7	8	6	4	1
1	2	6	4	9	5	8	3	7
7	8	4	3	1	6	2	9	5
2	7	8	5	3	4	1	6	9
9	6	1	8	2	7	4	5	3
5	4	3	1	6	9	7	8	2
6	3	5	7	4	2	9	1	8
8	9	7	6	5	1	3	2	4
4	1	2	9	8	3	5	7	6

NOTES:
. . . .
. . . .
. . . .
. . . .
. . . .
. . . .
. . . .

```
W C H X Q J J O H N G O O D M A N Y
S F H O V P N F K C V B H D S R E G
M C Z R A D L P X B K K D W R F C A
J I A N I G A M D Y B U K G A D A R
F D N R L S T N B Q R C V N Y A N U
D W J S L L T L X L H C I H Y N D W
R A O U R E A O U K S T T G I N I I
E Y H Q L P T A P D M R Q F W Y C L
W N N S Z E P T J H A D W W P D E L
B E M U M X C Y J C E Y G E R E B F
A J U A M A V L C O Z R G F D V E E
R O L G J L N M M L H N W P G I R R
R H A C H O A W Y E T A L A P T G R
Y N N Z A S N P Q U G O N Z L O E E
M S E K S E Y A S Q D L M S C K N L
O O Y I L Y P T H B S K A H S E E L
R N L H P P L V J H N P I A A O U N
E E D P L R M V V I W G H S N N H
M S E E H O H F M M I L A T G E K B
F B I L L M U R R A Y S L H U N U S
```

BONUS: CELEBRITIES THAT
HAVE HOSTED SNL FIVE OR
MORE TIMES

```
T K C E C I L T U R T L E I J Y P K
Y E M M I C H I G A N J F R O G Q T
C O Z H N R W I E T G F G Z N B O V
K N G O I H Q O P M S K V I N G A A
B I F B T N R G I V C I U C A M B U
E N O K I U J M K U M G N O S N K C
A H X Z C C Q O D U N W K L T R E I
K J Y X T W W A Y E G W G O Y G G S
Y E K L Q S S C P G A W Q N C O V G
B B S V H S O Y O H A Q G E A S G O
U X O W I S O D Y D R Z B L N S A O
Z U X L Q B E R D S Y Y N S A A B F
Z V E A Y I E R Y J N J M H S M B Y
A M Q A L N A F L I L I P U T E Y G
R M L R E Y N W A H K C F F A R G O
D P A H N E G S K Q X Q V F B Q O P
M H L R L E V A R M A X B L L K A H
C Y A K X S S M H G Z L B E J E T E
W B A W I T C H H A Z E L P M Z S R
G H W T B B L A R L R X I R Y F O S
```

NOTES:
. . . .
. . . .
. . . .
. . . .
. . . .
. . . .

BONUS: LESSER KNOW
WARNER BROS. CARTOON
CHARACTERS

PAGE 35

NOTES:
. . . .
. . . .
. . . .
. . . .
. . . .
. . . .
. . . .
. . . .
. . . .

START

FINISH

NOTES:

. . . .

. . . .

. . . .

. . . .

. . . .

. . . .

. . . .

BONUS: CELEBRITIES
THAT KATE HUDSON HAS
DATED

```
P D P D E R E K H O U G H Y Q R I E
H A Q M D L L O X L J D M W T A A H
E N Y M R Z E Y V N F A I M P T G R
A N U L H L L V B U L D P P N D I T
T Y E T H H H D C L G M W O L X I Q
H F M R L A N C E A R M S T R O N G
L U C A H K A B B X R L A K P S O I
E J N H B E W T S S I E D S D X A Y
D I Z D R E G E Q W U M A P B P L W
G S W D H I V S N I K E M U X H E A
E A Z T N Q S E P G S S S L J X R
R W T C A Y W R O J Y C C K X A R Z
R A F D N O A U O G F B O Z M L O L
M N L E B E M G I B W C T U T X D A
E A C E T R W J E B I H T B A P R M
L W I W K D H F U Y Q N X B E S I J
M D A X S H E P A R D I S F B A G G
U U N R K W H L S P F J J O W O U U
F Y N I C K J O N A S Z L A N X E B
F U S A Q B R U S G B X C O R K Z H
```

NOTES:

. . . .

. . . .

. . . .

. . . .

. . . .

. . . .

. . . .

. . . .

1	6	4	2	5	8	3	9	7
9	5	7	3	4	6	8	1	2
2	8	3	9	7	1	6	5	4
3	2	8	5	9	7	1	4	6
5	4	1	8	6	3	2	7	9
7	9	6	1	2	4	5	8	3
6	3	9	4	1	5	7	2	8
8	1	2	7	3	9	4	6	5
4	7	5	6	8	2	9	3	1

Word Search Grid:

```
S M A R T Y J O N E S N A N Y Z R E
S A E A L W A Y S D R E A M I N G T
F E T H U N D E R G U L C H V U E Z
U X A E S I L V E R C H A R M J M F
S W I H J A E R N F G F C F R C O Z
A M H P E V G A C O B O C A O A G C
I K A G O R C K O P C R G S F N K O
C H L Y J A O N U L Q I R F M I I G
H C A L I F O R N I A C H R O M E V
I S E J X U U K T S E H B I S A A S
P B T Y Y Y J O R A R S A P A L U U
E K H R Z U M J Y S X T R L Y K T P
G P F C E O J P H D B R B A Y I H E
A C T Z C E N F O F P I A P V N E R
S I T A C F T Q U C G K R H F G N S
U M I G D A A S S R B E O S B D T A
S G D O D R J K E H R W L R N O I V
O G R I N D S T O N E J O A S M C E
F N R P Z N F W Y F S N Z O N P F R
R E A L Q U I E T B Q E K H M I O Q
```

. . . .
. . . .
. . . .
. . . .
. . . .
. . . .

BONUS: HORSES THAT
HAVE WON THE KENTUCKY
DERBY

NOTES:
. . . .
. . . .
. . . .
. . . .
. . . .
. . . .
. . . .
. . . .

8	1	3	9	6	7	5	2	4
2	6	7	1	5	4	8	3	9
9	5	4	2	8	3	6	1	7
1	2	5	7	3	8	9	4	6
3	8	9	6	4	1	7	5	2
4	7	6	5	9	2	1	8	3
5	4	1	3	7	6	2	9	8
6	9	8	4	2	5	3	7	1
7	3	2	8	1	9	4	6	5

NOTES:

. . . .

. . . .

. . . .

. . . .

. . . .

. . . .

. . . .

. . . .

. . . .

START

FINISH

NOTES:

. . . .

. . . .

. . . .

. . . .

. . . .

. . . .

. . . .

. . . .

BONUS: EPISODE
TITLES OF THE TV SHOW
'THE OFFICE'

```
C G G N P Q Z D O Q Y Y P V E U L S
A I C O I U J R A S R U J L N G R Z
S L O V X R Y U E Q Q A L G T U Q S
U A C H Q O G G V X C A E P O I E T
A U K G S M Z T E K C X Y H C C C Y
L N T O Y L J E I E B D R R N T A M
F C A P G V Q S R E A E Y A C H S K
R H I Z E A T T M K T W L V O E I K
I P L F L W C I N F Q L V O M S N V
D A S R T U O N A I I R X Y P T O C
A R O R D W E G J E I G B I A I N H
Y T I O B K R D V F P K W L N N I A
K Y R C N S K R A M Y F N A Y G G I
R P Q F F U U F J K F S K M P B H R
V P Y U Q S O Z Q E T S S W I H T M
N E Y I L T H E C A R P E T C T J O
T K J I B S W J O B F A I R N W N D
G B A S K E T B A L L J R H I C H E
Q M K S K A V F N Y D D B T C R S L
E M Q R S U I T W A R E H O U S E A
```

7	9	6	4	3	8	1	2	5
5	8	4	6	2	1	3	7	9
1	2	3	9	7	5	8	6	4
6	1	8	3	9	2	4	5	7
2	3	5	7	1	4	6	9	8
4	7	9	5	8	6	2	3	1
9	5	1	2	4	3	7	8	6
3	4	7	8	6	9	5	1	2
8	6	2	1	5	7	9	4	3

NOTES:

NOTES:

BONUS: SPORTS DEMONSTRATED
AT THE OLYMPICS THAT NEVER
BECAME OFFICIAL

```
M W J K W F H U R L I N G D P H O P
Y Z Y C J N V P C L I M A N M H S E
W A R C D Q O Y B V X S E H D G R S
K W A T E R S K I I N G F X K L B A
N K L Z Q N Q L V Y M I R Y I I J P
F R O L L E R H O C K E Y F T D L A
R E B R E L O B A N D Y J L E I S L
B V O F Z H U A C J M G Z F N F L O
K Z U S M B G D Q L S A O P L G A O
R Y L F Z D A O Z N L U M D Y P V U
D N E V L Y Y V L B X X O H U I F U E
M N S L E Z Z F L T F L O O N B O T
A G T E N P I N B O W L I N G P V G
V N Q Z O G L B Q V J M Q U I D H X
H D G Q B U C G K C W Y T O X N F T
K L Y L M W P D C K E J A R U J G G
J T A S I P I G E O N R A C I N G V
S R U E E N S Z T H F G D B E N K F
S I E O I M G Z X R Y A E T D T V X
N S K I B A L L E T R J V H N I W E
```

NOTES:

. . . .

. . . .

. . . .

. . . .

. . . .

. . . .

BONUS: TOWN NAMES
IN THE NEW ENGLAND AREA
OF THE UNITED STATES

```
P F K W A U Y G U F I M K U M S X P
D W P V B G G E D L O L D L Y M E I
I O S E E D E J A B U K Q L E E G E
C O Z Y C O R N E R I A F I R G N H
R T S Q B R E A D L O A F T Q F I O
O K A B Q H A P P Y L A N D I C R M
L Q T A Z Y H G M M P I M M F V Y Z
D W A L K C P N U O A H O B R C L B
F E N D B N P F H R S X S U I S C E
U G S H L Z H W B W E S Q Z E K E L
R Y K E I C I V G W N Z U R N X M C
N Q I A S J K Y F K J T I P D I J H
A V N D S J G O D A P E T J S O P E
C Z G Z C T O L R E W A O N H K D R
E K D I O O A Y A H J T V G I W S T
V U O C R P G K M B W I I O P J U O
T Q M I N S N G J F M C L V S Q J W
X C I K E H Y M H L X K L H X H Y N
Q T A Q R A Q U O W I E E R T Z S Y
N W C H P M B X E N Z T U R X X Z E
```

NOTES:

. . . .

. . . .

. . . .

. . . .

. . . .

. . . .

BONUS: OSCAR AWARD
WINNING MOVIES—FOR
SOUND

```
M W Z X U J G Z F N S R H U G O T Y
O K T I T N N M U C O S Y I O B B W
V D V V Y G L N S Y U U V B I I U O S
C F T H E D A R K K N I G H T X H A
X A X I B I A E A W D Z O C P K E Q
H I U C M A N D Z N O O U B L U M C
K U K Q J R N C Q X F X Q X U L I O
A R C T P H Y M E W M K Q Y H O A E
R Y I K B D Y H R P E N R W U J N N
R W Q B T H E H U R T L O C K E R R
I X R N O R T H Y G A I K B N M H G
V F Q D C K U A C V L A O C V R A R
A H C J I X U I Z X S J H N H U P A
L F O R D V F E R R A R I H S B S V
K Y P L E R C W B C F D U N E B O I
X X N B S R Z Z X W H I P L A S H D T
T M A D M A X F U R Y R O A D M Y Y
R F Z Z U Y Z J O F A F R W L S G W
Q I L I O I Z Q K S K Y F A L L O G
C H D K D U N K I R K Y D M Q Q E V
```

PAGE 77

1	3	7	8	5	4	9	2	6
6	4	9	2	2	1	8	7	5
2	8	5	9	6	7	1	3	4
9	2	1	4	3	6	5	8	7
5	7	5	2	1	8	6	9	3
8	6	3	7	9	5	2	4	1
3	5	8	1	7	2	4	6	9
4	9	6	5	8	3	7	1	2
7	1	2	6	4	9	3	5	8

NOTES:

. . . .

. . . .

. . . .

. . . .

. . . .

. . . .

. . . .

. . . .

PAGE 81

NOTES:

. . . .

. . . .

. . . .

. . . .

. . . .

. . . .

. . . .

. . . .

. . . .

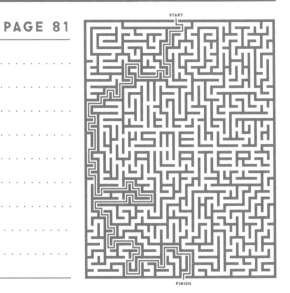

START

FINISH

NOTES:

. . . .
. . . .
. . . .
. . . .
. . . .
. . . .
. . . .
. . . .
. . . .

8	7	1	5	4	3	9	2	6
2	3	6	1	8	9	5	4	7
9	5	4	6	2	7	1	3	8
7	4	9	3	1	8	2	6	5
3	6	5	7	9	2	4	8	1
1	8	2	4	6	5	7	9	3
6	1	8	2	7	4	3	5	9
4	9	3	8	5	1	6	7	2
5	2	7	9	3	6	8	1	4

NOTES:

. . . .
. . . .
. . . .
. . . .
. . . .
. . . .
. . . .
. . . .

BONUS: CELEBRITIES
THAT HAVE HAD THEIR
OWN TALK SHOWS

```
D Z W Q N W E M F J M Z Z K G J A Q
B L A K M I S P S N O C D H E P T X
F Z Y H E N A K L S Z Y Y N O S D W
H I N L G R H B R Y P P Z K R R H X
A E E O A G C K Y M J L A Q G J Y E
F S B E N E Y Y X C T R J Y E K T E
I E R K M W V E D E Y E N D L C R N
T N A A U O E M N N R H E A O I O R
A C D R L Y H S A W A C L U P N H U
L R Y D L Y C F R A B S L W E N S O
N E R A A L Z O B Z A E A A Z O N B
E N L S L W S Y L N N R Y N O C I S
E N I H L P C X L A K D L D A Y T O
U E T I Y M D A E D S N I A X R R N
Q J A A W L I N S Y T A L S C R A O
U S N N U I C A S N K R K Y Q A M R
I I L J O D B E U O S F E K H H J A
K R Z U Z D K J R T V U X E J U J H
H K X T S P P I L I H P Y S U B N S
U O M F V V O A L A N T H I C K E U
```

```
M I N K A K E L L Y A Z E U R D B C
K R I S T I N C A V A L L A R I S P
J J H Q X J U B B I W X H D W L K I
P E Q J E S S I C A S I M P S O N R
R P N E T K A T Y P E R R Y K Q J X
B R A N G R Z U Q M H F U O H J U A
V P E G I T T A Y L O R S W I F T L
A O C N X F R A S H I D A J O N E S
N W L L E D E H T F T G D Z M G B C
E I Y V A E L R O G O X I P N E O A
S E Q V X I Z W L N Z F H A H Q Y M
S H S S V F T E G O A A U W E J E E
A T W M U R A G L H V M N W L W I R
C D M E X N Q D T L Q E I D M U S O
A X A Y S Q D S I A W V H T V X D N
R A B V V H S D W N S E L E R X W D
L J S S U U S F J C Z V G V A I I A
T I R B H A T X L F L C S E W I M A
O F R T C F A Z O K Q V V U R H T Z
N J E N N I F E R A N I S T O N S T
```

NOTES:

BONUS: CELEBRITIES
THAT JOHN MAYER HAS
DATED

NOTES:

4	9	8	7	3	6	1	2	5
3	5	1	8	2	4	6	9	7
2	7	6	5	9	1	4	3	8
1	4	9	6	5	3	8	7	2
8	2	3	1	7	9	5	6	4
7	6	5	4	8	2	3	1	9
5	1	2	9	6	8	7	4	3
6	3	7	2	4	5	9	8	1
9	8	4	3	1	7	2	5	6

NOTES:

. . . .
. . . .
. . . .
. . . .
. . . .
. . . .
. . . .
. . . .
. . . .

START

FINISH

```
N H X Y H Y A G J W F O R Y O U A E
T J J W Q D B R K R T S T N O Q E N
L H S B A T M A N X I L H T U Z P C
F U E Q N X I F D U K T E V G U F H
K Z U R U W L F F V I T G Y P O I A
D D R O A X C I W O I P O C Y P C O
Q J Q C L I M T E K Q L L R Y K L S
W C W C P O N I T C E I D Y A I N A
L O B H M A M B T Z M R E S P V Y N
J N P H H D J R O R A T X T K O D D
H T L W N I L I B W N A P A A B O D
A R A P A R A D E N C G E L N Q O I
V O N B L T V G R B I H R B Y Y F S
K V E M V Y A E J L P Q I A A Q U O
I E T I Q M H H U X A H E L F L K R
D R E J U I N I G K T Q N L D D B D
Q S A O J N T X M Q I D C J E R I E
E Y R O X D O T F R O V E G Q I E R
S S T F C U U M M K N J L U P K T N
L D H T H E B L A C K A L B U M C E
```

NOTES:

. . . .
. . . .
. . . .
. . . .
. . . .
. . . .

BONUS: TITLES OF ALBUMS
THAT WERE RELEASED
BY PRINCE

7	4	1	8	6	9	5	2	3
5	9	2	7	3	4	6	1	8
8	3	6	1	2	5	4	7	9
2	6	8	3	7	1	9	5	4
4	5	7	9	8	2	3	6	1
9	1	3	4	5	6	7	8	2
3	7	5	2	4	8	1	9	6
1	8	4	6	9	7	2	3	5
6	2	9	5	1	3	8	4	7

NOTES:

NOTES:

BONUS: CAST MEMBERS
OF THE MOVIE 'WET HOT
AMERICAN SUMMER'

NOTES:

. . . .
. . . .
. . . .
. . . .
. . . .
. . . .
. . . .
. . . .
. . . .
. . . .

START

FINISH

YOU   ARE   LIKE

SO   SMART   WOW

NOTES:

. . . .
. . . .
. . . .
. . . .
. . . .
. . . .
. . . .
. . . .
. . . .
. . . .

```
W C L T W S B L U E N O S E I P B V
V H Y S H Z J Y M Z O G C G Y S I Z
B I D D D E W D R O P P E R G A G M
E C A L B S C Q R V H X A Y S D C J
V A W B N T E A C F R Q E Y Y N H S
T G V P O R P O T S G N D G Q R E O
G O H I O U X K O S O A O N V O S C
F L W F D G E M Y L P V Z C T S S K
J I N J L G L A A G C A Y N Z A E D
U G E H E L T B D B K G J F F X O O
I H Q V J E G N U K N M O A V B L L
C T R J U B T M G P N C R T M R B L
E N E Q I U I C Y M I T T W W A O A
J D J C G I G G L E W A T E R S G E
O N I N E G O F A F H P R L S A Z E
I G P F K Y W B E A N S H O O T E R
N S K N O W Y O U R O N I O N S L G
T D N B G V I X X P U S B Q U V K L
C Y O N O C K P O D K Y N V Y E B P
H I J K Q R C E B U Z Z E R X X B J
```

NOTES:
. . . .
. . . .
. . . .
. . . .
. . . .
. . . .

BONUS: COMMON SLANG WORDS FROM THE 1920s

NOTES:
. . . .
. . . .
. . . .
. . . .
. . . .
. . . .
. . . .
. . . .
. . . .

5	3	2	8	4	6	9	1	7
4	6	7	3	1	9	5	2	8
1	8	9	7	2	5	3	4	6
7	4	5	1	8	2	6	9	3
8	9	1	4	6	3	7	5	2
6	2	4	5	9	7	4	8	1
2	7	6	9	5	1	8	3	4
3	5	8	2	7	4	1	6	9
9	1	4	6	3	8	2	7	5

NOTES:

. . . .

. . . .

. . . .

. . . .

. . . .

. . . .

. . . .

. . . .

BE — SURE — TO

DRINK — YOUR

OVALTINE

NOTES:

. . . .

. . . .

. . . .

. . . .

. . . .

. . . .

. . . .

```
S F G R A N D A D D Y P U R P L E O
N U B T M D X Z N D U B W A F A J R
M O P L D L U T M N M P J B T C L E
B W R E C Z I V I Z G N E W W O M L
Z L U T R Z K E E H F V V M W N Y T
X U U F H S G Q Q J E K X O U F I G
S M Z E L E I K Q U J W D H Q I H O
O K E R D A R L U O E I U H U D S L
U Y E Q P R X N V K W O U O J E L D
R M N R C N E K L E J Q N W U N K E
D I Q E O E F A T I R W D S M T H N
I Z R U U F D I M J G H A B E I J G
E P T E H U H K Y A T H A K N A C O
S N H M E W U E P X E Y T Z J L J A
E I I D V M E N Z V N O N S E S C T
L D P I N E A P P L E E X P R E S S
H M R B P D K I M A U I W O W I E B
L V F R U I T Y P E B B B L E S N U
T X O P J C Y H A O P J L Y L V O Q
S A C A P U L C O G O L D K Q W Z K
```

BONUS: NAMES OF
POPULAR STRAINS OF
MARIJUANA

PAGE 128

4	8	7	5	2	1	3	6	9
3	9	2	4	8	6	5	1	7
5	6	1	3	7	9	4	2	8
6	1	3	9	4	8	7	5	2
2	7	5	6	1	3	9	8	4
9	4	8	7	5	2	6	3	1
8	5	4	1	3	7	2	9	6
7	2	9	8	6	5	1	4	3
1	3	6	2	9	4	8	7	5

NOTES:
. . . .
. . . .
. . . .
. . . .
. . . .
. . . .
. . . .
. . . .
. . . .

PAGE 130

NOTES:
. . . .
. . . .
. . . .
. . . .
. . . .
. . . .
. . . .
. . . .
. . . .

START

FINISH

NOTES:

8	5	9	1	4	2	3	6	7
2	1	6	5	3	7	8	9	4
7	4	3	9	8	6	2	5	1
6	2	1	7	5	4	9	3	8
5	3	8	2	1	9	7	4	6
9	7	4	8	6	3	1	2	5
4	6	2	3	7	1	5	8	9
1	9	5	6	2	8	4	7	3
3	8	7	4	9	5	6	1	2

NOTES:

4	5	1	7	6	8	9	3	2
6	2	9	3	4	1	5	7	8
7	3	8	2	9	5	6	4	1
9	8	2	5	3	4	7	1	6
1	7	6	9	8	2	4	5	3
5	4	3	6	1	7	2	8	9
2	9	5	8	7	3	1	6	4
8	1	7	4	2	6	3	9	5
3	6	4	1	5	9	8	2	7

```
Q K U K V D P M N A G B X Q W W Y Z
I F F P P I S A D R O R O H U T O K
B K Y C H C P V R B O V O S U Q G Y
A M H A T P H E A W S S I O L D O T
W E I O J L P R R Y E K Y O S B E Z
F R T V L P M I P X S J B J N T Q C
N L F J I L I C A Q E L K A L E E C
A I G H N L Y K J R F D F R S C C R
F N C A B B R W O Q Y M P D Z W V V
I J E S T E R X O D C M V N V O V M
C H U E D H B W K O F K I G R L U B
P X A L U U Y B N V D C F C J F T W
U H C P A Y B A C K X I G O X M E O
Y G O O N N M D H Z Y Y P S A N U V
I J X E Y G U W X H I M D Q P N S S
J C L H N O W W Q E X D M G V Q V L
R W E A X I T J Z C W L E D N P C I
U S H M P W X E X H T P V G G L L D
N O A L A Z H C H A R L I E Q O I E
L R S T I N G E R M Z A C O U G A R
```

NOTES:

. . . .

. . . .

. . . .

. . . .

. . . .

. . . .

BONUS: FIGHTER PILOT
CALL SIGNS FROM THE
MOVIE 'TOP GUN'

NOTES:

. . . .

. . . .

. . . .

. . . .

. . . .

. . . .

. . . .

. . . .

. . . .

START

FINISH

NOTES:

. . . .

. . . .

. . . .

. . . .

. . . .

. . . .

. . . .

. . . .

. . . .

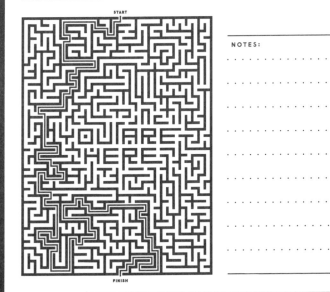

START

NOTES:

. . . .

. . . .

. . . .

. . . .

. . . .

. . . .

. . . .

. . . .

. . . .

FINISH

7	2	5	8	9	4	6	1	3
1	8	6	5	3	7	4	2	9
4	9	3	6	1	2	7	5	8
5	1	9	4	8	6	3	7	2
2	3	4	7	5	9	1	8	6
8	6	7	1	2	3	9	4	5
9	7	2	3	4	5	8	6	1
6	5	1	9	7	8	2	3	4
3	4	8	2	6	1	5	9	7

NOTES:

PAGE 160

NOTES:

1	8	2	5	6	3	7	4	9
9	6	5	4	7	2	1	8	3
7	4	3	1	9	8	5	2	6
4	2	9	7	1	5	3	6	8
3	1	6	8	4	9	2	7	5
8	5	7	3	2	6	4	9	1
2	3	8	6	5	4	9	1	7
6	9	1	2	3	7	8	5	4
5	7	4	9	8	1	6	3	2

NOTES:

. . . .

. . . .

. . . .

. . . .

. . . .

. . . .

. . . .

BONUS: BREAKFAST
CEREALS THAT HAVE BEEN
DISCONTINUED

```
A R A I N B O W B R I T E A Z G S P
Z C T S C O C O A H O O T S L W D M
N U Z A O P Q H M A G I C P U F F S
C D C A O H M C R A Z Y C O W P Y Y
S U E H I D D E N T R E A S U R E S
W P J E W A F F E L O S B I Q S W G
M K R C P W Y U M M Y M U M M Y J W
E M S I R S E Y G O M H F X Q E O D
Z N N R N Y B S C E O U B D D L U F
N C H C Q K P A A P M N I A L C J G
M H H U I S L V C Z A N S E Z K Z S
L O E S K J T E Z R F J F T R J V Y
I C J F Y E F R S A U E C V O H B H
G O J U A N C Y B P P N M B E N I P
C D F N I O B X N A A Z C J F V E I
D O F C L O E M R O J N Y H K A B S
H N P M E X P G Q C V E G I L J R Y
S U G A R K R I N K L E S L M J R K
T T M E V I P W S M N M O E E H A H
C S F C S Z J P Z Z H N Z N I S A I
```

NOTES:

. . . .

. . . .

. . . .

. . . .

. . . .

. . . .

. . . .

BONUS: NICKNAMES THAT
LESLIE KNOPE HAS GIVEN ANN
PERKINS IN 'PARKS & REC.'

```
D C T Q O O P S X Z V E P E A I X F
G R X B P O W E R F U L M U S K O X
Q Y K B A A U N I C O R N N U R S E
B I B E L S K L T I X O V J P S R O
M U Q A E A P P R A S B C B E Q U R
U F M U S S E S I U P B A L R P L U
S L A T C S O C C K A I R L F E E D
Q A L I E Y B J K E C G R Q E B B E
T N W F N M X P Y E E I Q V C Y R B
Z D P U T A K R M K U S U G T I E B
E M R L T N Z S I X N U O Z S I A N
K E K S R N N G N S I N E G U E K Z
Q R A P E E Q N X Y C G W M N J I L
P M U I E Q Q V B S O O Q Q F A N I
Y A K N S U I E M Y R D Z H L L G D
D I O S H I U V T R N D F E O P M Q
C D E T A N T J G U L E A D W A O R
T C A E R S R X V V M S Y W E L T N
O C L R K N A I B P B S T W R D H X
Y J O Z D D S A J Y P W Q K Q T Y J
```

THIS IS THE END OF THE BOOK.

COLOR THIS IN—AND THEN FIND SOMETHING
MORE PRODUCTIVE TO DO WITH YOUR LIFE.

BONUS FUN!
REACH OUT ON
INSTAGRAM AND
SAY HI.

SUMMER COCKTAILS

TRADITIONAL AND MODERN COCKTAILS
FOR EVERY OCCASION

LINDA DOESER

PHOTOGRAPHY BY CHRIS LINTON

Bath New York Singapore Hong Kong Cologne Delhi Melbourne

This edition published by Parragon in 2008

Parragon
Queen Street House
4 Queen Street
Bath BA1 1HE, UK

Created and produced for Parragon by The Bridgewater Book Company Ltd.

Cover by Talking Design

This edition produced by Design Principals

ISBN: 978-1-4054-7735-2

Printed in China

NOTE
*This book uses metric and imperial measurements. Follow the same units of
measurement throughout; do not mix metric and imperial. All spoon measurements
are level: teaspoons are assumed to be 5 ml and tablespoons are assumed to be 15 ml.
Unless otherwise stated, milk is assumed to be full fat, eggs and individual vegetables
such as potatoes are medium, and pepper is freshly ground black pepper.*

*The times given for each recipe are an approximate guide only. The preparation times
may differ according to the techniques used by different people and include chilling
and marinating times, where appropriate.*

*Recipes using raw or very lightly cooked eggs should be avoided by infants, the elderly,
pregnant women, convalescents and anyone suffering from an illness.*

Contents

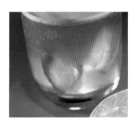

Introduction

Precisely where the word 'cocktail' came from is uncertain. A popular piece of folklore describes how a Mexican princess called Xoctl offered a mixed drink to an American visitor to her father's court who confused her name with that of the drink itself. Another suggestion is that the spoon used for mixing drinks reminded

mixed drinks have existed since ancient times and the first recognisable cocktail dates from about the sixteenth century. Indeed, many classics have been around for much longer than most people think. The bourbon-based Old Fashioned, for example, first appeared at the end of the eighteenth century. We know that the

imbibing racegoers of the docked tails of non-thoroughbred horses, called cocktails. There are many other flights of fancy, but modern etymologists mostly agree that the word derives from *coquetel*, a French, wine-based drink. Whatever the origins of the word cocktail,

word cocktail was already in use in 1809 in the United States and, thirty-five years later, when Charles Dickens described Major Pawkins as able to drink 'more rum-toddy, mint-julep, gin-sling, and cock-tail, than any private gentleman of his acquaintance', it had reached Britain, too. Popular among the style-conscious and wealthy in the United States, cocktails were served before dinner in the most exclusive houses and hotels until World

War I made them unfashionable. They have gone in and out of vogue ever since.

Following the war, young people, disillusioned by the elder generation and desperately seeking new experiences, pleasures, stimuli and styles, developed a taste for a new range of cocktails. Ironically, Prohibition in the United States

in the 1920s spurred on their development. Illegally produced liquor frequently tasted poisonous – and sometimes was – so its flavour needed to be disguised with fruit juices and mixers. No doubt, the naughtiness of drinking alcoholic cocktails also added to their appeal to the 'bright young things' of the time. The craze quickly crossed the Atlantic and the best hotels in London, Paris and Monte Carlo, where the quality

of gin and whisky was more consistent, soon boasted their own cocktail bars.

World War II brought an end to such revelry and, although drunk occasionally, cocktails remained out of style for decades until an exuberant renaissance in the 1970s. This resulted in another new generation of recipes, often featuring white rum and vodka, and tequila, which was just becoming known outside its native Mexico. Inevitably, the pendulum swung against cocktails again until recently. Now, once more, the cocktail shaker is essential equipment in every fashionable city bar.

Essentials

Making, serving and, above all, drinking cocktails should be fun. All you need is some basic equipment, a few ingredients and a sense of adventure.

Equipment

Classic cocktails are either shaken or stirred. A shaker is an essential piece of equipment, consisting of a container with an inner, perforated lid and an outer lid. Both lids are secured while the mixture is shaken, together with cracked ice, and then the cocktail is strained through the perforated lid into a glass.

A mixing glass is a medium-sized jug in which stirred cocktails can be mixed. It is usually made of uncoloured glass so you can see what you are doing.

A long-handled bar spoon is perfect for stirring and a small strainer prevents the ice cubes – used during mixing – finding their way into the cocktail glass. Some modern cocktails, including slushes, are made in a blender or food processor, so if you have one, by all means make use of it. Any cocktail that is made by shaking can also be made in a blender.

Measuring cups, sometimes called 'jiggers', and spoons are essential for getting the proportions right – guessing does not work. A corkscrew, bottle-opener and sharp knife are crucial.

Glasses

You can serve cocktails in any glasses you like. Small, V-shaped, stemmed glasses may be worth buying, but it is not essential to have a full range of Old fashioned, Highball, Collins glasses and so on. Tumblers, small tumblers and wine glasses cover most contingencies. As part of their appeal is visual, cocktails are best served in clear, uncut glass. Chill the glasses in the refrigerator to ensure cocktails are cold.

Ingredients

You can stock your bar over a period of time with the basics – it is not necessary to buy everything at once. A good, all-round selection of alcoholic drinks would include whisky, possibly Scotch and bourbon, brandy, gin, light and dark rum, triple sec, sweet and dry vermouth, vodka and tequila. You could also include Pernod, beer, and red and white wine. Keep champagne cocktails for special occasions. Select your stock according to your tastes – for example, if you never drink whisky, it would be extravagant to buy Scotch, Irish, Canadian, American blended and bourbon.

Standard mixers include soda water, sparkling mineral water, cola, ginger ale and tonic water. Freshly squeezed fruit juice is best, but when buying juice in a bottle or carton, avoid any with added sugar or extra 'padding'. Cranberry juice, for example, may be bulked with grape juice. Commercial brands of grapefruit, orange, cranberry, tomato juice and lime cordial are useful.

A good supply of fresh lemons, limes and oranges is essential. Fresh fruit is best, but if you use canned, buy it in natural juice rather than syrup, and drain well. Other useful garnishes and condiments include Angostura bitters, Worcestershire sauce and cocktail cherries. Finally, you can never have too much ice.

Techniques

Cracking and Crushing Ice

Store ice in the freezer until just before use. Cracked ice is used in both shaken and stirred cocktails. To crack ice, put ice cubes into a strong plastic bag and hit it against an outside wall, or put the ice between clean cloths on a sturdy surface and crush with a wooden mallet or rolling pin. Crushed ice is used in cocktails made in a blender. To crush ice, crack it as before but break it into much smaller pieces.

Frosting Glasses

Glasses can be frosted with sugar – or fine or coarse salt in the case of the Margarita or Salty Dog. Simply rub the rim of the glass with a wedge of lemon or lime, then dip the rim into a saucer of caster sugar or fine salt until it is evenly coated.

Making Sugar Syrup

To make sugar syrup, put 4 tablespoons water and 4 tablespoons caster sugar into a small saucepan and stir over a low heat until the sugar has dissolved. Bring to the boil, then continue to boil, without stirring, for 1–2 minutes. Cool, then refrigerate in a covered container for up to 2 weeks.

Shaken or Stirred?

To make a shaken cocktail, put fresh cracked ice into a cocktail shaker and pour over the other ingredients immediately. Secure the lids and shake vigorously for 10–20 seconds, until the outside of the shaker is coated in condensation. Strain into a glass and serve at once. To make a stirred cocktail, again use fresh cracked ice and pour over the ingredients immediately. Using a long-handled spoon, stir vigorously, without splashing, for 20 seconds, then strain into a glass and serve at once.

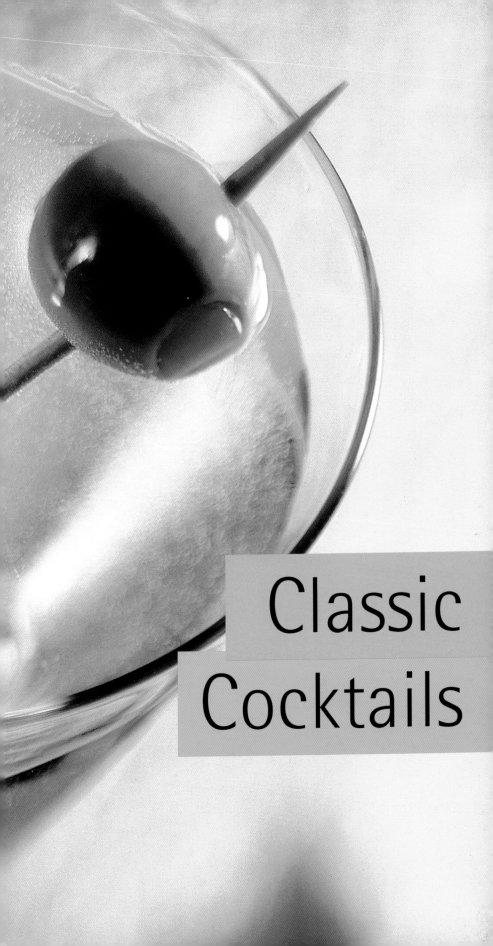

Classic
Cocktails

Classic Cocktail

This cannot lay claim to being the first or even the only classic, but it has all the characteristic hallmarks of sophistication associated with cocktails.

serves 1

wedge of lemon

1 tsp caster sugar

4–6 cracked ice cubes

2 measures brandy

½ measure clear Curaçao

½ measure Maraschino

½ measure lemon juice

lemon peel twist, to decorate

❶ Rub the rim of a chilled cocktail glass with the lemon wedge and then dip in the sugar to frost.

❷ Put the cracked ice into a cocktail shaker. Pour the brandy, Curaçao, Maraschino and lemon juice over the ice and shake vigorously until a frost forms.

❸ Strain into the frosted glass and decorate with the lemon twist.

Variations

A number of cocktails are the quintessential classics of their type and named simply after the main ingredient.

Champagne Cocktail: place a sugar cube in the bottom of a chilled champagne flute and dash with Angostura bitters to douse it. Fill the glass with chilled champagne and decorate with a twist of lemon.

Tequila Cocktail: put 4–6 cracked ice cubes into a cocktail shaker. Dash Angostura bitters over the ice and pour in 3 measures golden tequila, 1 measure lime juice and ½ measure grenadine. Shake vigorously until a frost forms, then strain into a chilled cocktail glass.

Brandy Cocktail: put 4–6 cracked ice cubes into a cocktail shaker. Dash Angostura bitters over the ice and pour in 2 measures brandy and ½ teaspoon sugar syrup (see page 7). Shake vigorously until a frost forms, then strain into a chilled cocktail glass and decorate with a twist of lemon.

Bartender's Tip

Maraschino is a sweet Italian liqueur made from cherries. It is usually white, but may also be coloured red. The white version is better for most cocktails, because it does not affect the appearance of the finished drink.

Sidecar

Cointreau is the best-known brand of the orange-flavoured liqueur known generically as triple sec. It is drier and stronger than Curaçao and is always colourless.

serves 1

4-6 cracked ice cubes
2 measures brandy
1 measure triple sec
1 measure lemon juice
orange peel twist, to decorate

❶ Put the ice into a cocktail shaker. Pour the brandy, triple sec and lemon juice over the ice and shake vigorously until a frost forms.
❷ Strain into a chilled glass and decorate with the orange peel twist.

Variations

Champagne Sidecar: make a Sidecar, but strain it into a chilled champagne flute and then top it up with chilled champagne.

Chelsea Sidecar: put 4-6 cracked ice cubes into a cocktail shaker. Pour 2 measures gin, 1 measure triple sec and 1 measure lemon juice over the ice. Shake vigorously until a frost forms, then strain into a chilled cocktail glass. Decorate with a lemon peel twist.

Boston Sidecar: put 4-6 cracked ice cubes into a cocktail shaker. Pour 1½

measures white rum, ½ measure brandy, ½ measure triple sec and ½ measure lemon juice over the ice and shake vigorously until a frost forms. Strain into a chilled cocktail glass and decorate with an orange peel twist.

Polish Sidecar: put 4-6 cracked ice cubes into a cocktail shaker. Pour 2 measures gin, 1 measure blackberry brandy and 1 measure lemon juice over the ice. Shake vigorously until a frost forms, then strain into a chilled cocktail glass. Decorate with a fresh blackberry.

Did you know?

You can buy 'ice cubes' made from soapstone. Place them in the freezer to chill and use as you would ice cubes. They will not dilute your cocktails and will last forever.

Stinger

Aptly named, this is a refreshing, clean-tasting cocktail to tantalise the taste buds and make you sit up and take notice. However, bear in mind that it packs a punch and if you have too many, you are likely to keel over.

serves 1

4–6 cracked ice cubes
2 measures brandy
1 measure white crème de menthe

❶ Put the ice cubes into a cocktail shaker. Pour the brandy and crème de menthe over the ice. Shake vigorously until a frost forms.
❷ Strain into a small, chilled highball glass.

Variations

Amaretto Stinger: put 4–6 cracked ice cubes into a cocktail shaker. Pour 2 measures amaretto and 1 measure white crème de menthe over the ice. Shake vigorously until a frost forms, then strain into a chilled cocktail glass.

Chocolate Stinger: put 4–6 cracked ice cubes into a cocktail shaker. Pour 1 measure dark crème de cacao and 1 measure white crème de menthe over the ice. Shake vigorously until a frost forms. Strain into a chilled cocktail glass.

Irish Stinger: put 4–6 cracked ice cubes into a cocktail shaker. Pour 1 measure Bailey's Irish Cream and 1 measure white crème de menthe over the ice. Shake vigorously until a frost forms, then strain into a chilled shot glass.

Did you know?

Bailey's Irish Cream is the world's top-selling liqueur and accounts for one per cent of Eire's export revenue.

American Rose

'A rose by any other name...' – this Oscar-winning cocktail has, rightly, inspired roses across the world. It is truly a thing of beauty and a joy forever.

serves 1

4–6 cracked ice cubes
1½ measures brandy
1 tsp grenadine
½ tsp Pernod
½ fresh peach, peeled and mashed
sparkling wine, to top up
fresh peach wedge, to decorate

❶ Put the cracked ice in a cocktail shaker. Pour the brandy, grenadine and Pernod over the ice and add the peach. Shake vigorously until a frost forms.

❷ Strain into a chilled wine goblet and top up with sparkling wine. Stir gently, then garnish with the peach wedge.

Variations

White Rose: put 4–6 cracked ice cubes into a cocktail shaker. Dash lemon juice over the ice and pour in 3 measures gin, 1 measure Maraschino and 1 measure orange juice. Shake until a frost forms. Strain into a chilled cocktail glass.

Jack Rose: put 4–6 cracked ice cubes into a cocktail shaker. Add 2 measures Calvados or applejack brandy, ½ measure lime juice and 1 teaspoon grenadine. Shake vigorously until a frost forms, then strain into a chilled cocktail glass.

English Rose: put 4–6 cracked ice cubes into a cocktail shaker. Dash lemon juice over the ice and pour in 2 measures gin, 2 measures dry vermouth and 1 measure apricot brandy. Shake until a frost forms.

Strain into a chilled cocktail glass.

Russian Rose: put 4–6 cracked ice cubes into a glass. Dash orange bitters over the ice and pour in 3 measures strawberry-flavoured vodka, ½ measure dry vermouth and ½ measure grenadine. Stir gently and strain into a chilled cocktail glass.

Bermuda Rose: put 4–6 cracked ice cubes into a cocktail shaker. Pour 2 measures gin, 2 teaspoons apricot brandy, 1 tablespoon lime juice and 2 teaspoons grenadine over the ice. Shake vigorously until a frost forms. Fill a chilled tumbler with crushed ice cubes. Strain the cocktail into the glass and top up with sparkling mineral water. Decorate with a lime slice.

Mint Julep

A julep is simply a mixed drink sweetened with syrup and it dates back to ancient times. The Mint Julep was probably first made in the United States, and is the traditional drink of the Kentucky Derby.

serves 1

leaves of 1 fresh mint sprig
1 tbsp sugar syrup (see page 7)
6–8 crushed ice cubes
3 measures bourbon whiskey
fresh mint sprig, to decorate

❶ Put the mint leaves and sugar syrup into a small, chilled glass and mash with a teaspoon. Add crushed ice to fill the tumbler, then add the bourbon.
❷ Decorate with the mint sprig.

Variations

Frozen Mint Julep: put 4–6 crushed ice cubes into a blender or food processor. Add 2 measures bourbon whiskey, 1 measure lemon juice, 1 measure sugar syrup (see page 7) and 6 fresh mint leaves. Process at low speed until slushy. Pour into a small, chilled tumbler and decorate with a fresh mint sprig.

Brandy Julep: fill a chilled tumbler with cracked ice. Add 2 measures brandy,

1 teaspoon sugar syrup (see page 7) and 4 fresh mint leaves. Stir well to mix and decorate with a fresh mint sprig and a slice of lemon. Serve with a straw.

Jocose Julep: put 4–6 crushed ice cubes into a blender or food processor. Pour 3 measures bourbon whiskey, 1 measure green crème de menthe, 1½ measures lime juice and 1 teaspoon sugar syrup (see page 7) over the ice. Add 5 fresh mint leaves. Process until smooth. Fill a chilled tumbler with cracked ice cubes and pour in the cocktail. Top up with sparkling mineral water and stir gently to mix. Decorate with a fresh mint sprig.

Did you know?

The word 'julep' is derived from Persian and came to us via Arabic. It means rose-water.

Whiskey Sour

Sours are short drinks, flavoured with lemon or lime juice. They can be made with almost any spirit, although Whiskey Sour was the original and, for many, is still the favourite.

serves 1

4–6 cracked ice cubes
2 measures American blended whiskey
1 measure lemon juice
1 tsp sugar syrup (see page 7)

To decorate

cocktail cherry

slice of orange

❶ Put the cracked ice into a cocktail shaker. Pour the whiskey, lemon juice and sugar syrup over the ice. Shake vigorously until a frost forms.

❷ Strain into a chilled cocktail glass and decorate with the cherry and orange slice.

Variations

Bourbon Sour: substitute bourbon for the whiskey and decorate with an orange slice.

Brandy Sour: substitute 2½ measures brandy for the blended whiskey.

Boston Sour: add 1 egg white to the ingredients and decorate with a cocktail cherry and a slice of lemon.

Polynesian Sour: put 4–6 cracked ice cubes into a cocktail shaker. Pour 2 measures white rum, ½ measure lemon juice, ½ measure orange juice and ½ measure guava juice over the ice. Shake vigorously until a frost forms, then pour into a chilled cocktail glass. Decorate with a slice of orange.

Fireman's Sour: put 4–6 cracked ice cubes into a cocktail shaker. Pour 2 measures white rum, 1½ measures lime juice, 1 tablespoon grenadine and

1 teaspoon sugar syrup (see page 7) over the ice. Shake until a frost forms. Strain into a cocktail glass and decorate with a cocktail cherry and a slice of lemon.

Strega Sour: put 4–6 cracked ice cubes into a cocktail shaker. Pour 2 measures gin, 1 measure Strega and 1 measure lemon juice over the ice. Shake vigorously until a frost forms. Strain into a cocktail glass and decorate with a slice of lemon.

Double Standard Sour: put 4–6 cracked ice cubes into a cocktail shaker. Pour 1½ measures blended American whiskey, 1½ measures gin, 1 measure lemon juice, 1 teaspoon grenadine and 1 teaspoon sugar syrup (see page 7) over the ice. Shake vigorously until a frost forms. Strain into a chilled cocktail glass and decorate with a cocktail cherry and a slice of orange.

Manhattan

Said to have been invented by Sir Winston Churchill's American mother, Jennie, the Manhattan is one of many cocktails named after places in New York. The centre of sophistication in the Jazz Age, the city is, once again, buzzing with cocktail bars for a new generation.

serves 1

4–6 cracked ice cubes

dash of Angostura bitters

3 measures rye whiskey

1 measure sweet vermouth

cocktail cherry, to decorate

❶ Put the cracked ice into a mixing glass. Dash the Angostura bitters over the ice and pour in the whiskey and vermouth. Stir well to mix.

❷ Strain into a chilled glass and decorate with the cherry.

City lights

Harlem Cocktail: put 4–6 cracked ice cubes into a cocktail shaker. Pour 2 measures gin, 1½ measures pineapple juice and 1 teaspoon Maraschino over the ice and add 1 tablespoon chopped fresh pineapple. Shake vigorously until a frost forms, then strain into a small, chilled tumbler.

Brooklyn: put 4–6 cracked ice cubes into a mixing glass. Dash Amer Picon and Maraschino over the ice and pour in 2 measures rye whiskey and 1 measure dry vermouth. Stir to mix, then strain into a chilled cocktail glass.

Broadway Smile: pour 1 measure chilled triple sec into a small, chilled tumbler. With a steady hand, pour 1 measure chilled crème de cassis on top,

without mixing, then pour 1 measure chilled Swedish Punsch on top, again without mixing.

Fifth Avenue: pour 1½ measures chilled dark crème de cacao into a small, chilled, straight-sided glass. With a steady hand, pour 1½ measures chilled apricot brandy on top, without mixing, then pour ¾ measure chilled single cream on top, again without mixing.

Coney Island Baby: put 4–6 cracked ice cubes into a cocktail shaker. Pour 2 measures peppermint schnapps and 1 measure dark crème de cacao over the ice. Shake vigorously until a frost forms. Fill a small, chilled tumbler with cracked ice and strain the cocktail over it. Top up with soda water and stir gently.

Old Fashioned

So ubiquitous is this cocktail that a small, straight-sided tumbler is known as an old-fashioned glass. It is a perfect illustration of the saying, 'Sometimes the old ones are the best.'

serves 1

sugar cube
dash of Angostura bitters
1 tsp water
2 measures bourbon or rye whiskey
4–6 cracked ice cubes
lemon peel twist, to decorate

❶ Place the sugar cube in a small, chilled Old Fashioned glass. Dash the bitters over the cube and add the water. Mash with a spoon until the sugar has dissolved.

❷ Pour the bourbon or rye whiskey into the glass and stir. Add the cracked ice cubes and decorate with the lemon twist.

'Not old, but mellow'

Brandy Old Fashioned: place a sugar cube in a small, chilled tumbler. Dash Angostura bitters over the sugar to douse and add a dash of water. Mash with a spoon until the sugar has dissolved, then pour in 3 measures brandy and add 4–6 cracked ice cubes. Stir gently and decorate with a lemon twist.

Old Etonian: put 4–6 cracked ice cubes into a mixing glass. Dash crème de noyaux and orange bitters over the ice and pour in 1 measure gin and 1 measure Lillet. Stir to mix, then strain into a chilled cocktail glass. Squeeze over a piece of orange peel.

Old Pal: put 4–6 cracked ice cubes into a cocktail shaker. Pour 2 measures rye whiskey, 1½ measures Campari and 1 measure sweet vermouth over the ice. Shake vigorously until a frost forms, then strain into a chilled cocktail glass.

Old Trout: put 4–6 cracked ice cubes into a cocktail shaker. Pour 1 measure Campari and 2 measures orange juice over the ice. Shake vigorously until a frost forms. Fill a tall glass with ice cubes and strain the cocktail over them. Top up with sparkling water and decorate with a slice of orange.

Old Pale: put 4–6 cracked ice cubes into a mixing glass. Pour 2 measures bourbon, 1 measure Campari and 1 measure dry vermouth over the ice. Stir well, then strain into a chilled cocktail glass. Squeeze over a piece of lemon peel.

Martini

For many, this is the ultimate cocktail. It is named after its inventor, Martini de Anna de Toggia, and not the famous brand of vermouth. The original version comprised equal measures of gin and vermouth, now known as a Fifty-fifty, but the proportions vary, up to the Ultra Dry Martini, when the glass is merely rinsed out with vermouth before the gin is poured in.

serves 1

4–6 cracked ice cubes
3 measures gin
1 tsp dry vermouth, or to taste
cocktail olive, to decorate

❶ Put the cracked ice cubes into a mixing glass. Pour the gin and vermouth over the ice and stir well to mix.
❷ Strain into a chilled cocktail glass and decorate with a cocktail olive.

Variations

Gibson: decorate with 2–3 cocktail onions, instead of an olive.
Vodka Martini: substitute vodka for the gin.
Tequini: put 4–6 cracked ice cubes into a mixing glass. Dash Angostura bitters over the ice and pour in 3 measures white tequila and ½ measure dry vermouth. Stir well to mix, strain into a chilled cocktail glass and decorate with a twist of lemon.

Dirty Martini: put 4–6 cracked ice cubes into a cocktail shaker. Pour 3 measures gin, 1 measure dry vermouth and ½ measure brine from a jar of cocktail olives over the ice. Shake vigorously until a frost forms. Strain into a chilled cocktail glass and decorate with a cocktail olive.
Saketini: put 4–6 cracked ice cubes into a cocktail shaker. Pour 3 measures gin and ½ measure Sake over the ice. Shake vigorously until a frost forms. Strain into a chilled cocktail glass and decorate with a twist of lemon peel.

Did you know?

Not only did James Bond always demand that his Martini should be shaken, not stirred, but his creator, Ian Fleming, also followed this practice.

Salty Dog

This is another cocktail that has changed since its invention. When it first appeared, gin-based cocktails were by far the most popular, but nowadays, a Salty Dog is more frequently made with vodka. You can use either spirit, but the cocktails will have different flavours.

serves 1

1 tbsp granulated sugar
1 tbsp coarse salt
lime wedge
6–8 cracked ice cubes
2 measures vodka
grapefruit juice, to top up

❶ Mix the sugar and salt in a saucer. Rub the rim of a chilled Collins glass with the lime wedge, then dip it in the sugar and salt mixture to frost.

❷ Fill the glass with cracked ice cubes and pour the vodka over them. Top up with grapefruit juice and stir to mix. Serve with a straw.

Variations

Bride's Mother: put 4–6 cracked ice cubes into a cocktail shaker. Pour 1½ measures sloe gin, 1 measure gin, 2½ measures grapefruit juice and ½ measure sugar syrup (see page 11) over the ice. Shake vigorously until a frost forms, then strain into a chilled cocktail glass.

A. J: put 4–6 cracked ice cubes into a cocktail shaker. Pour 1½ measures applejack or apple brandy, and 1 measure grapefruit juice over the ice. Shake vigorously until a frost forms, then strain into a chilled cocktail glass.

Midnight Sun: put 4–6 cracked ice cubes into a cocktail shaker. Pour 2 measures aquavit, 1 measure grapefruit juice and ¼ teaspoon grenadine over the ice. Shake vigorously until a frost forms, then strain into a chilled cocktail glass. Decorate with a slice of orange.

Blinker: put 4–6 cracked ice cubes into a cocktail shaker. Pour 2 measures rye whiskey, 2½ measures grapefruit juice and 1 teaspoon grenadine over the ice. Shake vigorously until a frost forms, then strain into a chilled cocktail glass.

Woodward: put 4–6 cracked ice cubes into a cocktail shaker. Pour 2 measures Scotch whisky, ½ measure dry vermouth and ½ measure grapefruit juice over the ice. Shake vigorously until a frost forms, then strain into a chilled cocktail glass.

White Lady

Simple, elegant, subtle and much more powerful than appearance suggests, this is the perfect cocktail to serve before an al fresco summer dinner.

serves 1

4-6 cracked ice cubes
2 measures gin
1 measure triple sec
1 measure lemon juice

❶ Put the ice into a cocktail shaker. Pour the gin, triple sec and lemon juice over the ice. Shake vigorously until a frost forms.
❷ Strain into a chilled cocktail glass.

Variations

Green Lady: put 4-6 cracked ice cubes into a cocktail shaker. Dash lime juice over the ice and pour in 2 measures gin and 1 measure green Chartreuse. Shake vigorously until a frost forms, then strain into a chilled cocktail glass.

Creole Lady: put 4-6 cracked ice cubes into a mixing glass. Pour 2 measures bourbon, 1½ measures Madeira and 1 teaspoon grenadine over the ice. Stir well to mix, then strain into a chilled cocktail glass. Decorate with cocktail cherries.

Perfect Lady: put 4-6 cracked ice cubes into a cocktail shaker. Pour 2 measures gin, 1 measure peach brandy and 1 measure lemon juice over the ice. Add 1 teaspoon egg white. Shake until a frost forms. Strain into a chilled cocktail glass.

Apricot Lady: put 4-6 cracked ice cubes into a cocktail shaker. Pour 1½ measures white rum, 1 measure apricot brandy, 1 tablespoon lime juice, ½ teaspoon triple sec over the ice and add 1 egg white.

Shake vigorously until a frost forms. Half fill a small, chilled tumbler with cracked ice. Strain the cocktail over the ice and decorate with a slice of orange.

Blue Lady: put 4-6 cracked ice cubes into a cocktail shaker. Pour 2½ measures blue Curaçao, 1 measure white crème de cacao and 1 measure single cream over the ice. Shake until a frost forms, then strain into a chilled cocktail glass.

My Fair Lady: put 4-6 cracked ice cubes into a cocktail shaker. Dash strawberry liqueur over the ice, pour in 2 measures gin, 1 measure orange juice, 1 measure lemon juice and add 1 egg white. Shake vigorously until a frost forms. Strain into a chilled cocktail glass.

Shady Lady: put 4-6 cracked ice cubes into a cocktail shaker. Dash lime juice over the ice and pour in 3 measures tequila, 1 measure apple brandy and 1 measure cranberry juice. Shake until a frost forms. Strain into a chilled cocktail glass.

Tom Collins

This cocktail combines gin, lemon juice and soda water to make a cooling long drink. This is a venerable cocktail, but the progenitor of several generations of the Collins family of drinks, scattered across the globe, was the popular John Collins cocktail.

serves 1

5–6 cracked ice cubes
3 measures gin
2 measures lemon juice
½ measure sugar syrup (see page 7)
soda water, to top up
slice of lemon, to decorate

❶ Put the cracked ice into a cocktail shaker. Pour the gin, lemon juice and sugar syrup over the ice. Shake vigorously until a frost forms.
❷ Strain into a tall, chilled tumbler and top up with soda water. Decorate with a slice of lemon.

Variations

John Collins: substitute Dutch gin or genever for the dry gin.

Mick Collins: substitute Irish whiskey for the gin.

Pierre Collins: substitute brandy for the gin.

Pedro Collins: substitute white rum for the gin.

Colonel Collins: substitute bourbon for the gin.

Mac Collins: substitute Scotch whisky for the gin.

Ivan Collins: substitute vodka for the gin and decorate with a slice of orange and a cocktail cherry.

Belle Collins: crush 2 fresh mint sprigs and place in a tall, chilled tumbler. Add 4–6 crushed ice cubes and pour in 2 measures gin, 1 measure lemon juice and 1 teaspoon sugar syrup (see page 7).

Top up with sparkling water, stir gently and decorate with a fresh mint sprig.

Juan Collins: half fill a chilled tumbler with cracked ice and pour in 2 measures white tequila, 1 measure lemon juice and 1 teaspoon sugar syrup (see page 7). Top up with sparkling mineral water and stir gently. Decorate with a cocktail cherry.

Country Cousin Collins: put 4–6 crushed ice cubes into a blender. Dash orange bitters over the ice and pour in 2 measures apple brandy, 1 measure lemon juice and ½ teaspoon sugar syrup (see page 7). Blend at medium speed for 10 seconds. Pour into a chilled tumbler and top up with sparkling water. Stir gently and decorate with a slice of lemon.

Singapore Sling

In the days of the British Empire, the privileged would gather in the relative cool of the evening to refresh parched throats and gossip about the day's events at exclusive clubs. Those days are long gone, but a Singapore Sling is still the ideal thirst-quencher on hot summer evenings.

serves 1

10–12 cracked ice cubes
2 measures gin
1 measure cherry brandy
1 measure lemon juice
1 tsp grenadine
soda water, to top up

To decorate
lime peel
cocktail cherries

❶ Put 4–6 cracked ice cubes into a cocktail shaker. Pour the gin, cherry brandy, lemon juice and grenadine over the ice. Shake vigorously until a frost forms.

❷ Half fill a chilled highball glass with cracked ice cubes and strain the cocktail over them. Top up with soda water and decorate with lime peel and cocktail cherries.

Variations

Sweet Singapore Sling: put 4–6 cracked ice cubes into a cocktail shaker. Dash lemon juice over the ice and pour in 1 measure gin and 2 measures cherry brandy. Shake vigorously until a frost forms. Half fill a chilled tumbler with cracked ice cubes and strain the cocktail over them. Top up with soda water and decorate with cocktail cherries.

Gin Sling: put 1 teaspoon sugar in a mixing glass. Add 1 measure lemon juice and 1 teaspoon water and stir until the sugar has dissolved. Pour in 2 measures gin and stir to mix. Half fill a small, chilled tumbler with ice and strain the cocktail over it. Decorate with an orange twist.

Whiskey Sling: put 1 teaspoon sugar in a mixing glass. Add 1 measure lemon juice and 1 teaspoon water and stir until the sugar has dissolved. Pour in 2 measures American blended whiskey and stir to mix. Half fill a small, chilled tumbler with ice and strain the cocktail over it. Decorate with an orange twist.

Long Island Iced Tea

Like many other classics, this cocktail dates from the days of the American Prohibition when it was drunk from tea cups in an unconvincing attempt to fool the FBI that it was a harmless beverage. It started out life as a simple combination of vodka coloured with a dash of cola, but has evolved into a more elaborate, but no less potent, concoction.

serves 1

10–12 cracked ice cubes

2 measures vodka

1 measure gin

1 measure white tequila

1 measure white rum

½ measure white crème de menthe

2 measures lemon juice

1 tsp sugar syrup (see page 7)

cola, to top up

wedge of lime or lemon, to decorate

❶ Put 4–6 cracked ice cubes into a cocktail shaker. Pour the vodka, gin, tequila, rum, crème de menthe, lemon juice and sugar syrup over the ice. Shake vigorously until a frost forms.

❷ Half fill a tall, chilled tumbler with cracked ice cubes and strain the cocktail over them. Top up with cola and decorate with the lime or lemon wedge.

Brewing up

Artillery Punch (serves 30): pour 1 litre/ 1¾ pints bourbon, 1 litre/1¾ pints red wine, 1 litre/1¾ pints strong, black tea, 475 ml/ 17 fl oz dark rum, 250 ml/9 fl oz gin, 250 ml/9 fl oz apricot brandy, 4 measures lemon juice, 4 measures lime juice and 4 tablespoons sugar syrup (see page 7) in a large bowl. Refrigerate for 2 hours. To serve, place a large block of ice in a punch bowl. Pour the punch over the ice and decorate with thinly sliced lemon and lime.

Did you know?

In 1920, there were about 15,000 bars in New York. Following the introduction of Prohibition in 1920, the number of illegal speakeasies rocketed to some 32,000.

Piña Colada

One of the younger generation of classics, this became popular during the cocktail revival of the 1980s and has remained so ever since.

serves 1

4–6 crushed ice cubes
2 measures white rum
1 measure dark rum
3 measures pineapple juice
2 measures coconut cream
pineapple wedges, to decorate

❶ Put the crushed ice into a blender and add the white rum, dark rum, pineapple juice and coconut cream. Blend until smooth.

❷ Pour, without straining, into a tall, chilled glass and decorate with pineapple wedges speared on a cocktail stick.

Variations

Lighten Up Piña Colada: put 4–6 cracked ice cubes into a cocktail shaker. Pour 2 measures white rum, 2 measures Malibu and 3 measures pineapple juice over the ice. Shake vigorously until a frost forms. Half fill a small, chilled tumbler with cracked ice cubes and strain the cocktail over them. Decorate with a pineapple slice.

Amigos Piña Colada (to serve 4): put 10–12 crushed ice cubes into a blender and add 250 ml/9 fl oz white rum, 300 ml/10 fl oz pineapple juice, 5 measures coconut cream, 2 measures dark rum and 2 measures single cream. Blend until smooth. Pour, without straining, into tall, chilled tumblers and decorate with pineapple wedges speared on cocktail sticks.

Strawberry Colada: put 4–6 crushed ice cubes into a blender and add 3 measures golden rum, 4 measures pineapple juice, 1 measure coconut cream and 6 hulled strawberries. Blend until smooth, then pour, without straining, into a tall, chilled tumbler. Decorate with pineapple wedges and strawberries speared on a cocktail stick.

Banana Colada: put 4–6 crushed ice cubes into a blender and add 2 measures white rum, 4 measures pineapple juice, 1 measure Malibu and 1 peeled and sliced banana. Blend until smooth, then pour, without straining, into a tall, chilled tumbler and serve with a straw.

Acapulco

This is one of many cocktails that has changed from its original recipe over the years. To begin with, it was always rum-based and did not include any fruit juice. Nowadays, it is increasingly made with tequila, because this has become better known outside its native Mexico.

serves 1

10–12 cracked ice cubes
2 measures white rum
½ measure triple sec
½ measure lime juice
1 tsp sugar syrup (see page 7)
1 egg white
sprig of fresh mint, to decorate

❶ Put 4–6 cracked ice cubes into a cocktail shaker. Pour the rum, triple sec, lime juice and sugar syrup over the ice and add the egg white. Shake vigorously until a frost forms.
❷ Half fill a chilled highball glass with cracked ice cubes and strain the cocktail over them. Decorate with the mint sprig.

Variations

Acapulco Gold: put 4–6 cracked ice cubes into a cocktail shaker. Pour 1 measure golden tequila, 1 measure golden rum, 2 measures pineapple juice, 1 measure coconut cream and 1 measure grapefruit juice over the ice. Shake vigorously until a frost forms. Half fill a small, chilled tumbler with cracked ice cubes and strain the cocktail over them.

Acapulco Clam Digger: put 4–6 cracked ice cubes into a tall tumbler. Dash Tabasco sauce, Worcestershire sauce and lemon juice over the ice and pour in 1½ measures white tequila, 3 measures tomato juice and 3 measures clam juice. Add 2 teaspoons horseradish sauce. Stir well to mix, decorate with a slice of lime and serve with a straw.

Did you know?

Rum owes its origin to Christopher Columbus, who is said to have planted the first sugar cane in the islands of the Caribbean.

Daiquiri

Daiquiri is a town in Cuba, where this drink was said to have been invented in the early part of the twentieth century. A businessman had run out of imported gin and so had to make do with the local drink – rum – which, at that time, was of unreliable quality. To ensure that his guests would find it palatable he mixed it with other ingredients. This classic has since given rise to almost innumerable variations.

serves 1

4–6 cracked ice cubes
2 measures white rum
¾ measure lime juice
½ tsp sugar syrup (see page 7)

❶ Put the cracked ice cubes into a cocktail shaker. Pour the rum, lime juice and sugar syrup over the ice. Shake vigorously until a frost forms.
❷ Strain into a chilled cocktail glass.

Variations

Derby Daiquiri: put 4–6 crushed ice cubes into a blender and add 2 measures white rum, 1 measure orange juice, ½ measure triple sec and ½ measure lime juice. Blend until smooth, then pour, without straining, into a chilled cocktail glass.

Banana Daiquiri: put 4–6 crushed ice cubes into a blender and add 2 measures white rum, ½ measure triple sec, ½ measure lime juice, ½ measure single cream, 1 teaspoon sugar syrup (see page 7) and ¼ peeled and sliced banana. Blend until smooth, then pour the mixture, without straining, into a chilled goblet and decorate with a slice of lime.

Peach Daiquiri: put 4–6 crushed ice cubes into a blender and add 2 measures white rum, 1 measure lime juice, ½ teaspoon sugar syrup (see page 7) and ½ peeled, stoned and chopped peach. Blend until smooth, then pour, without straining, into a chilled goblet.

Passionate Daiquiri: put 4–6 cracked ice cubes into a cocktail shaker. Pour 2 measures white rum, 1 measure lime juice and ½ measure passion fruit syrup over the ice. Shake vigorously until a frost forms. Strain into a chilled cocktail glass and decorate with a cocktail cherry.

Bartender's Tip
For other Daiquiri variations, see page 66.

Cuba Libre

The 1960s and 1970s saw the meteoric rise in popularity of this simple, long drink, perhaps because of highly successful marketing by Bacardi brand rum, the original white Cuban rum (now produced in the Bahamas) and Coca-Cola, but more likely because rum and cola seem to be natural companions.

serves 1

4-6 cracked ice cubes
2 measures white rum
cola, to top up
wedge of lime, to decorate

❶ Half fill a highball glass with cracked ice cubes. Pour the rum over the ice and top up with cola.

❷ Stir gently to mix and decorate with a lime wedge.

Other Cuban classics

Bacardi Cocktail: put 4-6 cracked ice cubes into a cocktail shaker. Pour 2 measures Bacardi rum, 1 measure grenadine and 1 measure fresh lime juice over the ice. Shake vigorously until a frost forms. Strain into a chilled cocktail glass.

Brandy Cuban: half fill a chilled tumbler with cracked ice cubes. Pour 1½ measures brandy and ½ measure lime juice over the ice. Top up with cola and stir gently. Decorate with a slice of lime.

Cuban: put 4-6 cracked ice cubes into a cocktail shaker. Pour 2 measures brandy, 1 measure apricot brandy, 1 measure lime juice and 1 teaspoon white rum over the ice. Shake vigorously until a frost forms. Strain into a chilled cocktail glass.

Cuban Special: put 4–6 cracked ice cubes into a cocktail shaker. Pour 2 measures rum, 1 measure lime juice, 1 tablespoon pineapple juice and 1 teaspoon triple sec over the ice. Shake until a frost forms. Strain into a chilled cocktail glass and decorate with a pineapple wedge.

Did you know?

Britain's Royal Navy continued to provide sailors with a daily rum ration until 1969 although, by then, the quantity had been reduced from the original 300 ml/10 fl oz.

Zombie

The individual ingredients of this cocktail, including liqueurs and fruit juices, vary considerably from one recipe to another, but all zombies contain a mixture of white, golden and dark rum in a range of proportions.

serves 1

4-6 crushed ice cubes

2 measures dark rum

2 measures white rum

1 measure golden rum

1 measure triple sec

1 measure lime juice

1 measure orange juice

1 measure pineapple juice

1 measure guava juice

1 tbsp grenadine

1 tbsp orgeat

1 tsp Pernod

To decorate

sprig of fresh mint

pineapple wedges

❶ Put the crushed ice cubes into a blender and add the three rums, triple sec, lime juice, orange juice, pineapple juice, guava juice, grenadine, orgeat and Pernod. Blend until smooth.

❷ Pour, without straining, into a tall, chilled Collins glass and decorate with the mint sprig and pineapple wedges.

Variations

Walking Zombie: put 4-6 cracked ice cubes into a cocktail shaker. Pour 1 measure white rum, 1 measure golden rum, 1 measure dark rum, 1 measure apricot brandy, 1 measure lime juice, 1 measure pineapple juice and 1 teaspoon sugar syrup (see page 7) over the ice. Shake vigorously until a frost forms. Half fill a chilled tumbler with cracked ice cubes and strain the cocktail over them. Decorate with orange and lemon slices.

Zombie Prince: put 4-6 cracked ice cubes into a mixing glass. Dash Angostura bitters over the ice, pour in 1 measure white rum, 1 measure golden rum, 1 measure dark rum, ½ measure lemon juice, ½ measure orange juice and ½ measure grapefruit juice and add 1 teaspoon brown sugar. Stir to mix well, then strain into a tall, chilled tumbler.

Bartender's Tip

Orgeat is an almond-flavoured syrup. If you can't find it, you could substitute the same amount of amaretto, which is more widely available.

Mai Tai

For some reason, this cocktail always inspires elaborate decoration with paper parasols, a selection of fruit and spirals of citrus rind – sometimes so much so that you can be in danger of stabbing your nose on a cocktail stick when you try to drink it. If you want to go completely over the top with decorations – and why not – serving the drink with one or two long, colourful straws might be a good idea.

serves 1

4–6 cracked ice cubes

2 measures white rum

2 measures dark rum

1 measure clear Curaçao

1 measure lime juice

1 tbsp orgeat

1 tbsp grenadine

❶ Put the cracked ice cubes into a cocktail shaker. Pour the white and dark rums, Curaçao, lime juice, orgeat and grenadine over the ice. Shake vigorously until a frost forms.

❷ Strain into a chilled Collins glass and decorate with the paper parasol, pineapple and cherries, adding an orchid, if desired.

To decorate

paper parasol

slices of pineapple

cocktail cherries

orchid, optional

Other decorated cocktails

Generally speaking, you can decorate cocktails in any way you like – or not at all, if you prefer. There are some, however, that are traditionally served in a particular way. The Martini and the Gibson (see page 26), for example, are differentiated only because the former is decorated with a cocktail olive, while the latter is always served with a cocktail onion.

Horse's Neck: hang a long spiral of lemon rind over the rim of a tall, chilled tumbler. Fill the glass with cracked ice and pour 2 measures American blended whiskey over the ice. Top up with ginger ale and stir.

Ultimate Beefeater Martini: put 4–6 cracked ice cubes into a mixing glass. Dash dry vermouth over the ice and pour in 1 measure Beefeater gin. Stir well and strain the mixture into a chilled cocktail glass. Decorate with a sliver of fillet steak.

Margarita

The traditional way to drink tequila is to shake a little salt on the back of your hand between the thumb and forefinger and, holding a wedge of lime or lemon, lick the salt, suck the fruit and then down a shot of tequila in one. This cocktail, attributed to Francisco Morales and invented in 1942 in Mexico, is a more civilised version.

serves 1

lime wedge
coarse salt
4–6 cracked ice cubes
3 measures white tequila
1 measure triple sec
2 measures lime juice
slice of lime, to decorate

❶ Rub the rim of a chilled cocktail glass with the lime wedge and then dip in a saucer of coarse salt to frost.

❷ Put the cracked ice cubes into a cocktail shaker. Pour the tequila, triple sec and lime juice over the ice. Shake vigorously until a frost forms.

❸ Strain into the prepared glass and decorate with the lime slice.

Variations

Frozen Margarita: put 6–8 cracked ice cubes into a blender and add 2 measures white tequila, 1 measure lime juice and $1/2$ measure triple sec. Blend at low speed until slushy. Pour, without straining, into a chilled cocktail glass and decorate with a slice of lime.

Blue Margarita: frost the rim of a chilled cocktail glass using a lime wedge and coarse salt (as above). Put 4–6 cracked ice cubes into a cocktail shaker. Pour 2 measures white tequila, 1 measure blue Curaçao, $1^1/2$ measures lime juice and 1 tablespoon triple sec over the ice. Shake vigorously until a frost forms. Strain into the prepared glass and decorate with a slice of lime.

Margarita Impériale: put 4–6 cracked ice cubes into a cocktail shaker. Dash clear Curaçao over the ice and pour in 1 measure white tequila, 1 measure Mandarine Napoléon and 1 measure lemon juice. Shake vigorously until a frost forms. Strain into a chilled cocktail glass.

Peach Margarita: frost the rim of a chilled cocktail glass using a lime wedge and coarse salt (as above). Put 4–6 cracked ice cubes into a cocktail shaker. Pour 2 measures white tequila, 2 measures lime juice, $1/2$ measure peach liqueur and 1 tablespoon triple sec over the ice. Shake vigorously until a frost forms, then strain into the prepared glass. Decorate with a fresh peach slice.

Tequila Sunrise

This is one cocktail you shouldn't rush when making, otherwise you will spoil the attractive sunrise effect as the grenadine slowly spreads through the orange juice.

serves 1

4–6 cracked ice cubes
2 parts white tequila
orange juice, to top up
1 measure grenadine

❶ Put the cracked ice cubes into a chilled highball glass. Pour the tequila over the ice and top up with the orange juice. Stir well to mix.

❷ Slowly pour in the grenadine and serve with a straw.

Variations

Blinding Sunrise: put 4–6 cracked ice cubes into a cocktail shaker. Pour 1 measure white tequila, 1 measure vodka, 3 measures orange juice and 1 teaspoon triple sec over the ice. Shake vigorously until a frost forms. Half fill a tumbler with cracked ice cubes and strain the cocktail over them. Slowly pour in 1 measure grenadine.

Pacific Sunrise: put 4–6 cracked ice cubes into a cocktail shaker. Dash Angostura bitters over the ice and pour in 1 measure white tequila, 1 measure blue Curaçao and 1 measure lime juice. Shake vigorously until a frost forms, then strain into a chilled cocktail glass.

Mint Sunrise: put 4–6 cracked ice cubes into a chilled tumbler. Pour 1½ measures Scotch whisky, ½ measure brandy and ½ measure clear Curaçao over the ice and stir gently. Decorate with a fresh mint sprig and a slice of lemon.

Did you know?

The global popularity of tequila took producers by surprise. The agave plant from which it is made takes 8–10 years to mature: due to this long maturation time, and cultivation problems that subsequently developed, a severe shortage arose by the year 2000, which resulted in rocketing prices and a lucrative trade in 'cactus rustling'.

Bloody Mary

This classic cocktail was invented in 1921 at the legendary Harry's Bar in Paris. There are numerous versions – some much hotter and spicier than others. Ingredients may include horseradish sauce in addition to or instead of Tabasco sauce, more or less tomato juice, and lime juice instead of lemon. Sometimes the glass is decorated with a sprig of mint. Whatever the version, all experts agree that it is essential to use the highest-quality ingredients.

serves 1

4–6 cracked ice cubes
dash of Worcestershire sauce
dash of Tabasco sauce
2 measures vodka
6 measures tomato juice
juice of ½ lemon
pinch of celery salt
pinch of cayenne pepper

To decorate
celery stick with leaves
slice of lemon

❶ Put the cracked ice into a cocktail shaker. Dash the Worcestershire sauce and Tabasco sauce over the ice and pour in the vodka, tomato juice and lemon juice. Shake vigorously until a frost forms.

❷ Strain into a tall, chilled glass, add a pinch of celery salt and a pinch of cayenne and decorate with a celery stick and a slice of lemon.

Variations

Bloody Maria: substitute 2 measures white tequila for the vodka and add 1 teaspoon horseradish sauce and a pinch of ground coriander. Decorate with a lime wedge.

Cold and Clammy Bloody Mary: substitute 3 measures clam juice for 3 of the measures of tomato juice and decorate with a spring onion curl.

Bullshot: substitute 4 measures chilled beef stock for the tomato juice and season with salt and freshly ground black pepper.

Moscow Mule

This cocktail came into existence through a happy coincidence during the 1930s. An American bar owner had overstocked ginger beer, and a representative of a soft drinks company invented the Moscow Mule to help him out.

serves 1

10–12 cracked ice cubes
2 measures vodka
1 measure lime juice
ginger beer, to top up
slice of lime, to decorate

❶ Put 4–6 cracked ice cubes into a cocktail shaker. Pour the vodka and lime juice over the ice. Shake vigorously until a frost forms.

❷ Half fill a chilled highball glass with cracked ice cubes and strain the cocktail over them. Top up with ginger beer. Decorate with a slice of lime.

Other stubborn drinks

Delft Donkey: make a Moscow Mule but substitute gin for the vodka.

Mississippi Mule: put 4–6 cracked ice cubes into a cocktail shaker. Pour 2 measures gin, ½ measure crème de cassis and ½ measure lemon juice over the ice. Shake vigorously until a frost forms, then strain into a small, chilled tumbler.

Mule's Hind Leg: put 4–6 cracked ice cubes into a cocktail shaker. Pour ½ measure apricot brandy, ½ measure apple brandy, ½ measure Bénédictine, ½ measure gin and ½ measure maple syrup over the ice. Shake vigorously until a frost forms, then strain into a chilled cocktail glass.

Jamaica Mule: put 4–6 cracked ice cubes into a cocktail shaker. Pour 2 measures white rum, 1 measure dark rum, 1 measure golden rum, 1 measure Falernum and 1 measure lime juice over the ice. Shake vigorously until a frost forms, then strain the mixture into a tall, chilled tumbler. Top up with ginger beer and then decorate with some pineapple wedges and crystallised ginger.

Screwdriver

Always use freshly squeezed orange juice to make this refreshing cocktail – it is just not the same with bottled juice. This simple, classic cocktail has given rise to numerous and increasingly elaborate variations.

serves 1

6–8 cracked ice cubes
2 measures vodka
orange juice, to top up
slice of orange, to decorate

❶ Fill a chilled highball glass with cracked ice cubes. Pour the vodka over the ice and top up with orange juice.
❷ Stir well to mix and decorate with a slice of orange.

Variations

Cordless Screwdriver: pour 2 measures chilled vodka into a shot glass. Dip a wedge of orange into caster sugar. Down the vodka in one go and suck the orange.

Creamy Screwdriver: put 4–6 crushed ice cubes into a blender and add 2 measures vodka, 6 measures orange juice, 1 egg yolk and $\frac{1}{2}$ teaspoon sugar syrup (see page 7). Blend until smooth. Half fill a tall, chilled tumbler with cracked ice cubes and pour the cocktail over them without straining.

Harvey Wallbanger: make a Screwdriver, then float 1 measure Galliano on top by pouring it gently over the back of a teaspoon.

Slow Screw: substitute sloe gin for the vodka.

Bartender's Tip
Galliano is a honey- and vanilla-flavoured liqueur from Italy. It is sold in tall thin bottles, so bars store it on a top shelf up against the wall to avoid knocking it over.

Did you know?

The Harvey Wallbanger is named after a California surfer who took such prodigious delight in drinking Screwdrivers topped with a Galliano float that he ricocheted from wall to wall on leaving the bar.

Kir

As with the best mustard, crème de cassis production is centred on the French city of Dijon. This cocktail is named in commemoration of a partisan and mayor of the city, Félix Kir.

serves 1

4–6 cracked ice cubes
2 measures crème de cassis
white wine, to top up
twist of lemon peel, to decorate

❶ Put the crushed ice cubes into a chilled wine glass. Pour the crème de cassis over the ice.

❷ Top up with chilled white wine and stir well. Decorate with the lemon twist.

Wine toppers

Kir Royale: substitute champagne for the white wine.

Osborne (named after Queen Victoria's Isle of Wight residence and apparently a favourite tipple of Her Majesty's): pour 3 measures claret and 1 measure Scotch whisky into a goblet and stir to mix.

Bellini (created at Harry's Bar, Venice, and named after the Renaissance artist): fill a goblet with crushed ice and dash over grenadine. Pour in 1 measure peach juice, then top up with chilled champagne. Decorate with a peeled, fresh peach slice.

Bellinitini: put 4–6 cracked ice cubes into a cocktail shaker. Pour in 2 measures vodka, 1 measure peach schnapps and 1 measure peach juice.

Shake vigorously until a frost forms, then strain into a chilled goblet. Top up with chilled champagne.

Rikki-Tikki-Tavi: put a sugar cube into a chilled champagne flute and dash Angostura bitters over it until red but still intact. Pour in 1 teaspoon brandy and 1 teaspoon clear Curaçao and top up with chilled champagne.

Champagne Pick-me-up: put 4–6 cracked ice cubes into a cocktail shaker. Dash grenadine over the ice and then pour in 2 measures brandy, 1 measure orange juice and 1 measure lemon juice. Shake vigorously until a frost forms. Strain the mixture into a wine glass and then top up with chilled champagne.

Buck's Fizz

Invented at Buck's Club in London, the original was invariably made with Bollinger champagne and it is true that the better the quality of the champagne, the better the flavour.

serves 1

2 measures chilled champagne

2 measures chilled orange juice

❶ Pour the champagne into a chilled champagne flute, then pour in the orange juice.

Variations

Duck's Fizz: substitute Canard-Duchêne champagne for the Bollinger.

Mimosa: pour the orange juice into the flute and then the champagne. Stir gently. You can use sparkling white wine instead of champagne.

Black Velvet: pour 300 ml/10 fl oz chilled champagne or sparkling wine and 300 ml/10 fl oz chilled stout into a chilled tumbler at the same time. Do not stir.

Soyer au Champagne: put 1 scoop vanilla ice cream into a wine glass and add ¼ teaspoon brandy, ¼ teaspoon triple sec and ¼ teaspoon Maraschino. Stir to mix, then top up with chilled champagne. Stir gently and decorate with a cocktail cherry.

Champagne Cup: pour ½ measure brandy and ½ measure clear Curaçao into a chilled wine glass. Add 1 ice cube and top up with champagne. Decorate with a sprig of fresh mint and a slice of orange.

Spritzer: fill a wine glass with cracked ice cubes and pour in 3 measures white wine. Top up with soda water or sparkling mineral water and decorate with a twist of lemon peel.

Did you know?

In spite of his ruthless ambition and Prussian earnestness, Otto von Bismarck must have had a more frivolous side to his nature because he is reputed to have created the Black Velvet.

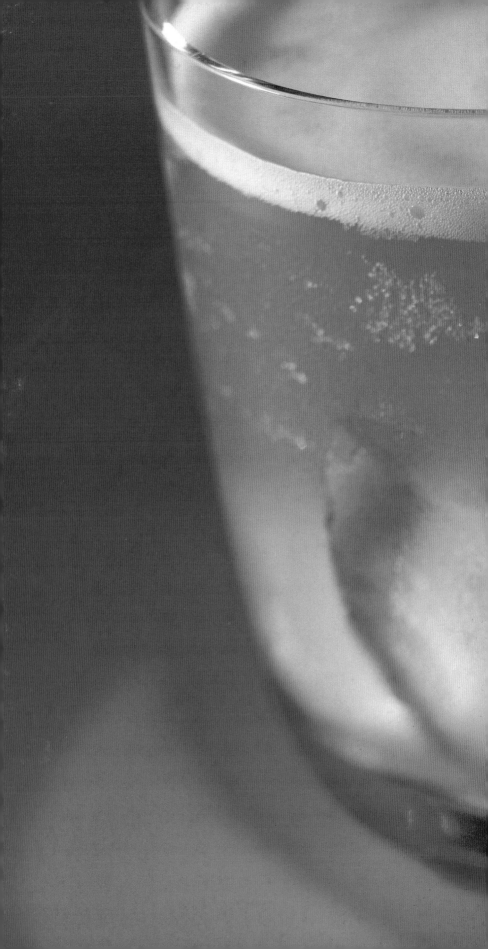

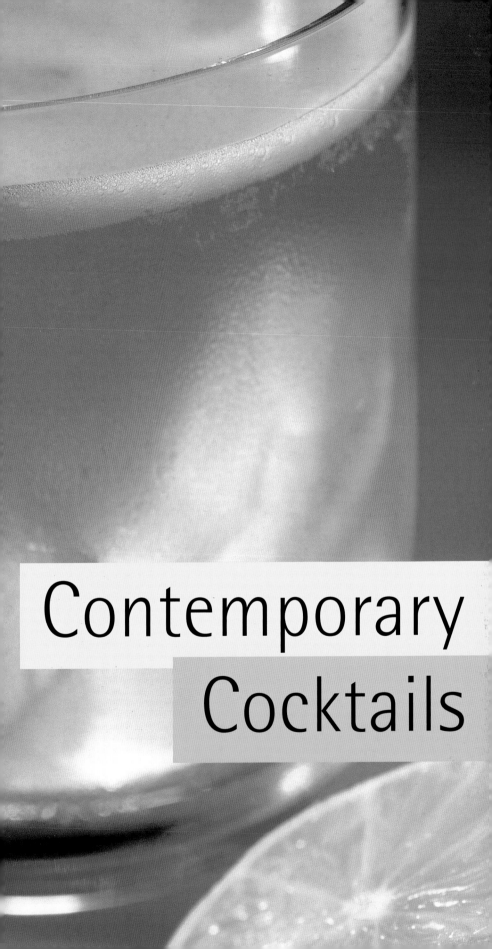

Contemporary
Cocktails

Frozen Daiquiri

One of the great classic cocktails, the Daiquiri (see page 42) has moved on. It's not just mixed with fresh fruit or unusual ingredients, it's entered the twenty-first century with a whole new future, as slushes take on a leading role in fashionable cocktail bars.

serves 1

6 crushed ice cubes
2 measures white rum
1 measure lime juice
1 tsp sugar syrup (see page 7)
slice of lime, to decorate

❶ Put the crushed ice into a blender and add the rum, lime juice and sugar syrup. Blend until slushy.

❷ Pour into a chilled champagne flute and decorate with the lime slice.

Variations

Frozen Pineapple Daiquiri: put 6 crushed ice cubes into a blender and add 2 measures white rum, 1 measure lime juice, ½ teaspoon pineapple syrup and 60 g/2 oz finely chopped fresh pineapple. Blend until slushy, then pour into a chilled cocktail glass. Decorate with pineapple wedges.

Frozen Mint Daiquiri: put 6 crushed ice cubes into a blender and add 2 measures white rum, ½ measure lime juice, 1 teaspoon sugar syrup (see page 7) and 6 fresh mint leaves. Blend until slushy, then pour into a chilled cocktail glass.

Frozen Strawberry Daiquiri: put 6 crushed ice cubes into a blender and add 2 measures white rum, 1 measure lime juice, 1 teaspoon sugar syrup (see page 7) and 6 fresh or frozen strawberries. Blend until slushy. Pour into a chilled cocktail glass. Decorate with a strawberry.

Frozen Peach Daiquiri: put 6 crushed ice cubes into a blender. Add 2 measures white rum, 1 measure lime juice, 1 teaspoon sugar syrup (see page 7) and ½ peeled, stoned and chopped peach. Blend until slushy. Pour into a chilled cocktail glass. Decorate with a slice of peach.

Tequila Slammer

Slammers, also known as shooters, are currently very fashionable. The idea is that you pour the different ingredients directly into the glass, without stirring (some slammers form colourful layers). Cover the top of the glass with one hand to prevent spillage, then slam the glass on the bar or a table to mix and drink the cocktail down in one. It is essential to use a strong glass that is unlikely to break under such treatment.

serves 1

1 measure white tequila
1 measure lemon juice
chilled sparkling wine, to top up

❶ Put the tequila and lemon juice into a chilled glass and stir to mix. Top up with sparkling wine.

❷ Cover the glass with your hand and slam.

'Those little shooters, how I love to drink them down...'

Alabama Slammer: put 4–6 cracked ice cubes into a mixing glass. Pour 1 measure Southern Comfort, 1 measure amaretto and ½ measure sloe gin over the ice and stir to mix. Strain into a shot glass and add ½ teaspoon lemon juice. Cover and slam.

B52: pour 1 measure chilled dark crème de cacao into a shot glass. With a steady hand, gently pour in 1 measure chilled Bailey's Irish Cream to make a second layer, then gently pour in 1 measure chilled Grand Marnier. Cover and slam.

B52 (second version): pour 1 measure chilled Kahlúa into a shot glass. With a steady hand, gently pour in 1 measure chilled Bailey's Irish Cream to make a second layer, then gently pour in 1 measure chilled Grand Marnier. Cover and slam.

Banana Slip: pour 1 measure chilled crème de banane into a shot glass. With a steady hand, gently pour in 1 measure chilled Bailey's Irish Cream to make a second layer. Cover and slam.

Wild Night Out

Tequila has a reputation for being an extraordinarily potent spirit, but most commercially exported brands are the same standard strength as other spirits, such as gin or whisky. 'Home-grown' tequila or its close relative, *mescal*, may be another matter.

serves 1

4–6 cracked ice cubes
3 measures white tequila
2 measures cranberry juice
1 measure lime juice
soda water, to top up

❶ Put the cracked ice cubes into a cocktail shaker. Pour the tequila, cranberry juice and lime juice over the ice. Shake vigorously until a frost forms. ❷ Half fill a chilled highball glass with cracked ice cubes and strain the cocktail over them. Add soda water to taste.

The wild bunch

Buttafuoco: put 4–6 cracked ice cubes into a cocktail shaker. Pour 2 measures white tequila, ½ measure Galliano, ½ measure cherry brandy and ½ measure lemon juice over the ice. Shake vigorously until a frost forms. Half fill a tumbler with cracked ice cubes and strain the cocktail over them. Top up with soda water and decorate with a cocktail cherry.

Magna Carta: rub the rim of a wine glass with a wedge of lime, then dip in caster sugar to frost. Put 4–6 cracked ice cubes into a mixing glass. Pour 2 measures white tequila and 1 measure triple sec over the ice and stir well to mix. Strain into the prepared glass and top up with chilled sparkling wine.

Tequila Fizz: put 4–6 cracked ice cubes into a cocktail shaker. Pour 3 measures white tequila, 1 measure grenadine and 1 measure lime juice over the ice and add 1 egg white. Shake vigorously until a frost forms. Half fill a chilled tumbler with cracked ice cubes and strain the cocktail over them. Top up with ginger ale.

Changuirongo: half fill a tall, chilled tumbler with cracked ice cubes. Pour 2 measures white tequila over the ice and top up with ginger ale. Stir gently and decorate with a slice of lime.

Carolina

White tequila is most commonly used for mixing cocktails, but some require the more mellow flavour of the amber-coloured, aged tequilas, which are known as golden tequila or *añejo*.

serves 1

4–6 cracked ice cubes
3 measures golden tequila
1 tsp grenadine
1 tsp vanilla essence
1 measure single cream
1 egg white

To decorate
ground cinnamon
cocktail cherry

❶ Put the cracked ice cubes into a cocktail shaker. Pour the tequila, grenadine, vanilla and cream over the ice and add the egg white. Shake vigorously until a frost forms.
❷ Strain into a chilled cocktail glass. Sprinkle with cinnamon and decorate with a cocktail cherry.

The golden touch

Grapeshot: put 4–6 cracked ice cubes into a cocktail shaker. Pour 2 measures golden tequila, 1 measure clear Curaçao and 1½ measures white grape juice over the ice and shake vigorously until a frost forms. Strain into a chilled cocktail glass.

Montezuma: put 4–6 crushed ice cubes into a blender and add 2 measures golden tequila, 1 measure Madeira and 1 egg yolk. Blend until smooth, then pour into a chilled cocktail glass.

Chapala: put 4–6 cracked ice cubes into a cocktail shaker. Pour 2 measures golden tequila, 2 measures orange juice, 1 measure lime juice, ½ measure triple sec and ½ measure grenadine over the ice. Shake vigorously until a frost forms. Half fill a chilled tumbler with cracked ice cubes and strain the cocktail over them.

Piñata: put 4–6 cracked ice cubes into a cocktail shaker. Pour 2 measures golden tequila, 1 measure crème de banane and 1½ measures lime juice over the ice and shake vigorously until a frost forms. Strain the mixture into a chilled cocktail glass.

Crocodile

This is certainly a snappy cocktail with a bit of bite. However, it probably gets its name from its spectacular colour – Midori, a Japanese melon-flavoured liqueur, which is a startling shade of green.

serves 1

4–6 cracked ice cubes

2 measures vodka

1 measure triple sec

1 measure Midori

2 measures lemon juice

❶ Put the cracked ice cubes into a cocktail shaker. Pour the vodka, triple sec, Midori and lemon juice over the ice. Shake vigorously until a frost forms.

❷ Strain into a chilled cocktail glass.

Variations

Alligator: put 4–6 cracked ice cubes into a cocktail shaker. Pour 2 measures vodka, 1 measure Midori, ½ measure dry vermouth and ¼ teaspoon lemon juice over the ice. Shake vigorously until a frost forms. Strain into a chilled cocktail glass.

Melon Ball: put 4–6 cracked ice cubes into a mixing glass. Pour 2 measures vodka, 2 measures Midori and 4 measures pineapple juice over the ice and stir well to mix. Half fill a chilled tumbler with cracked ice cubes and strain the cocktail over them. Decorate with a melon wedge.

Melon Balls: put 4–6 cracked ice cubes into a cocktail shaker. Pour 1 measure vodka, 1 measure Midori and 1 measure pineapple juice over the ice. Shake vigorously until a frost forms, then strain into a chilled cocktail glass.

Melon State Balls: put 4–6 cracked ice cubes into a cocktail shaker. Pour 2 measures vodka, 1 measure Midori and 2 measures orange juice over the ice cubes. Shake vigorously until a frost forms, then strain the mixture into a chilled cocktail glass.

Vodga

As a rule, classic cocktails based on vodka were intended to provide the kick of an alcoholic drink with no tell-tale signs on the breath and they were usually fairly simple mixes of fruit juice, sodas and other non-alcoholic flavourings. By contrast, contemporary cocktails based on vodka often include other aromatic and flavoursome spirits and liqueurs, with vodka adding extra strength.

serves 1

4–6 cracked ice cubes
2 measures vodka
1 measure Strega
½ measure orange juice

❶ Put the cracked ice cubes into a cocktail shaker. Pour the vodka, Strega and orange juice over the ice. Shake vigorously until a frost forms.
❷ Strain into a chilled cocktail glass.

Variations

Golden Frog: put 4–6 crushed ice cubes into a blender and add 1 measure vodka, 1 measure Strega, 1 measure Galliano and 1 measure lemon juice. Blend until slushy, then pour into a chilled cocktail glass.

Genoese: put 4–6 cracked ice cubes into a cocktail shaker. Pour 1 measure vodka, 1 measure grappa, ½ measure Sambuca and ½ measure dry vermouth over the ice. Shake vigorously until a frost forms, then strain into a chilled cocktail glass.

White Spider: put 4–6 cracked ice cubes into a mixing glass. Pour 1 measure vodka and 1 measure white crème de menthe over the ice. Stir well to mix, then strain into a chilled cocktail glass.

Tailgate: put 4–6 cracked ice cubes into a mixing glass. Dash orange bitters over the ice and pour in 2 measures vodka, 1 measure green Chartreuse and 1 measure sweet vermouth. Stir well to mix, then strain into a chilled cocktail glass.

Full Monty

The expression 'full monty', meaning not holding anything back, has been around for a long time, but was given a new lease of life by the highly successful British film of the same title. However, you can keep your clothes on when mixing and drinking this cocktail.

serves 1

4–6 cracked ice cubes
1 measure vodka
1 measure Galliano
grated ginseng root, to decorate

❶ Put the cracked ice cubes into a cocktail shaker. Pour the vodka and Galliano over the ice. Shake vigorously until a frost forms.

❷ Strain into a chilled cocktail glass and sprinkle with grated ginseng root.

Cinematic cocktails

Back to the Future: put 4–6 cracked ice cubes into a cocktail shaker. Pour 2 measures gin, 1 measure slivovitz and 1 measure lemon juice over the ice. Shake vigorously until a frost forms. Strain into a chilled cocktail glass.

Star Wars: put 4–6 cracked ice cubes into a cocktail shaker. Pour 2 measures gin, 2 measures lemon juice, 1 measure Galliano and 1 measure crème de noyaux over the ice. Shake vigorously until a frost forms. Strain into a chilled cocktail glass.

Titanic: put 4–6 cracked ice cubes into a cocktail shaker. Pour 3 measures Mandarine Napoléon and 2 measures vodka over the ice. Shake vigorously until a frost forms. Half fill a chilled tumbler with cracked ice cubes and strain the cocktail over them. Top up with sparkling mineral water.

Last Mango in Paris: put 4–6 cracked ice cubes into a blender and add 2 measures vodka, 1 measure crème de framboise, 1 measure lime juice, ½ peeled, stoned and chopped mango and 2 halved strawberries. Blend until slushy. Pour into a chilled goblet and decorate with a slice of lime and a strawberry.

What the Hell

Cheer yourself up when you are at a loose end, or when everything seems to have gone wrong, with this simple but delicious concoction.

serves 1

4-6 cracked ice cubes
dash of lime juice
1 measure gin
1 measure apricot brandy
1 measure dry vermouth
twist of lemon peel, to decorate

❶ Put the cracked ice cubes into a mixing glass. Dash the lime juice over the ice and pour in the gin, apricot brandy and vermouth. Stir well to mix.

❷ Strain into a chilled cocktail glass and decorate with a twist of lemon peel.

Silly questions and answers

Why Not: put 4-6 cracked ice cubes into a mixing glass. Dash lemon juice over the ice. Pour in 2 measures gin, 1 measure peach brandy and 1 measure Noilly Prat. Stir to mix. Strain into a chilled cocktail glass.

Is This All: put 4-6 cracked ice cubes into a cocktail shaker. Pour 2 measures lemon vodka, 1 measure triple sec and 1 measure lemon juice over the ice and add 1 egg white. Shake until a frost forms. Strain into a chilled cocktail glass.

What The Dickens: pour 2 measures gin into a heatproof tumbler and stir in 1½ teaspoons icing sugar. Top up with hot water.

This Is It: put 4-6 cracked ice cubes into a cocktail shaker. Pour 2 measures gin, 1 measure triple sec and 1 measure lemon juice over the ice and add 1 egg white. Shake vigorously until a frost forms, then strain the mixture into a chilled cocktail glass.

Did you know?

French vermouth, of which Noilly Prat is the leading brand, is almost always dry, whereas sweet red vermouth is still the most popular type in Italy, although all the well-known brands – Martini, Cinzano and Gancia – also include a dry version. Each firm keeps its own formula secret.

Non-alcoholic
Cocktails

Lip Smacker

So many delicious ingredients are available today that non-alcoholic cocktails really have come into their own. This one has all the kick of an alcoholic cocktail.

serves 1

4–6 crushed ice cubes

1 small tomato, peeled, deseeded and chopped

1 measure orange juice

2 tsp lime juice

1 spring onion, chopped

1 small, fresh, red chilli, deseeded and chopped

pinch of caster sugar

pinch of salt

dash of Tabasco sauce

To decorate

slice of lime and a chilli rosette (see below)

❶ Put the crushed ice, tomato, orange juice, lime juice, spring onion and chilli in a blender and process until smooth.

❷ Pour into a chilled glass, and stir in sugar, salt and Tabasco sauce. Decorate with a lime slice and a chilli rosette. To make a rosette, use a sharp knife to make 5 or 6 cuts 1 cm/ ½ inch from the stalk end to the tip of a long, thin chilli. Place in iced water for 30 minutes, until fanned out.

Variations

Hot Lips: substitute the flesh of ¼ small avocado for the tomato and a deseeded and chopped green chilli for the red chilli.
Open Prairie Oyster: dash Tabasco sauce and white wine vinegar into a wine glass and pour in 1 teaspoon Worcestershire sauce and 1 measure tomato juice. Stir gently and add 1 egg yolk. Drink down in one, without breaking the egg yolk.

Did you know?

Sun-ripened tomatoes have a much sweeter and more concentrated flavour than those grown under glass or in polytunnels. Home-grown varieties are best, but those sold on the vine are a good buy.

Little Prince

Sparkling apple juice is a particularly useful ingredient in non-alcoholic cocktails because it adds flavour and colour, as well as fizz. Try using it as a substitute for champagne in non-alcoholic versions of such cocktails as Buck's Fizz (see page 62).

serves 1

4–6 cracked ice cubes
1 measure apricot juice
1 measure lemon juice
2 measures sparkling apple juice
twist of lemon peel, to decorate

❶ Put the cracked ice cubes into a mixing glass. Pour the apricot juice, lemon juice and apple juice over the ice and stir well.
❷ Strain into a chilled highball glass and decorate with the lemon twist.

An apple a day

Apple Frazzle: put 4–6 cracked ice cubes into a cocktail shaker. Pour 4 measures apple juice, 1 teaspoon sugar syrup (see page 7) and ½ teaspoon lemon juice over the ice. Shake vigorously until a frost forms. Strain into a chilled tumbler and top up with sparkling mineral water.

Bite of the Apple: put 4–6 crushed ice cubes into a blender and add 5 measures apple juice, 1 measure lime juice, ½ teaspoon orgeat and 1 tablespoon apple sauce or apple purée. Blend until smooth, then pour into a chilled tumbler. Sprinkle with ground cinnamon.

Prohibition Punch (to serve 25): pour 900 ml/1½ pints apple juice, 350 ml/ 12 fl oz lemon juice and 125 ml/4 fl oz sugar syrup (see page 7) into a large jug. Add cracked ice cubes and 2.25 litres/ 4½ pints ginger ale. Stir gently to mix. Serve in chilled tumblers, decorated with slices of orange and with straws.

Red Apple Sunset: put 4–6 cracked ice cubes into a cocktail shaker. Dash grenadine over the ice and pour in 2 measures apple juice and 2 measures grapefruit juice. Shake until a frost forms. Strain into a chilled cocktail glass.

Grapefruit Cooler

This is a wonderfully refreshing drink that is ideal for serving at a family barbecue. Start making this at least two hours before you want to serve it to allow plenty of time for the mint to infuse in the syrup.

serves 6

60 g/2 oz fresh mint

2 measures sugar syrup (see page 7)

475 ml/17 fl oz grapefruit juice

4 measures lemon juice

about 30 cracked ice cubes

sparkling mineral water, to top up

sprigs of fresh mint, to decorate

❶ Crush the fresh mint leaves and place in a small bowl. Add the sugar syrup and stir well. Set aside for at least 2 hours to macerate, mashing the mint with a spoon from time to time.

❷ Strain the syrup into a jug and add the grapefruit juice and lemon juice. Cover with clingfilm and chill in the refrigerator for at least 2 hours, until required.

❸ To serve, fill six chilled Collins glasses with cracked ice. Divide the cocktail between the glasses and top up with sparkling mineral water. Decorate with fresh mint sprigs.

Cool it

Bright Green Cooler (serves 1): put 4–6 cracked ice cubes into a cocktail shaker. Pour 3 measures pineapple juice, 2 measures lime juice and 1 measure green peppermint syrup over the ice. Shake the mixture vigorously until a frost forms. Half fill a tall chilled tumbler with cracked ice cubes and then strain the cocktail over them. Top up with ginger ale and then decorate with a slice of cucumber and a slice of lime.

Did you know?

There is a green-skinned grapefruit variety called 'Sweetie' that is less sharp than the yellow-skinned fruits. Pink grapefruit is also slightly milder in flavour.

Shirley Temple

This is one of the most famous of classic non-alcoholic cocktails. Shirley Temple Black became a respected diplomat, but this cocktail dates from the days when she was an immensely popular child film star in the 1930s.

serves 1

8–10 cracked ice cubes

2 measures lemon juice

½ measure grenadine

½ measure sugar syrup (see page 7)

ginger ale, to top up

To decorate

slice of orange

cocktail cherry

❶ Put 4–6 cracked ice cubes into a cocktail shaker. Pour the lemon juice, grenadine and sugar syrup over the ice and shake vigorously.

❷ Half fill a small, chilled glass with cracked ice cubes and strain the cocktail over them. Top up with ginger ale. Decorate with an orange slice and a cocktail cherry.

Other classics

St Clements: put 6–8 cracked ice cubes into a chilled tumbler. Pour 2 measures orange juice and 2 measures bitter lemon over the ice. Stir gently and decorate with a slice of orange and a slice of lemon.

Black and Tan: pour 150 ml/5 fl oz chilled ginger ale into a chilled tumbler. Add 150 ml/5 fl oz chilled ginger beer. Do not stir. Decorate with a wedge of lime.

Tea Punch: put 4–6 cracked ice cubes into a mixing glass. Pour 3 measures cold

black tea, 3 measures orange juice, 3 measures sparkling apple juice and 1½ measures lemon juice over the ice. Stir well to mix, then pour into a tall, chilled tumbler. Decorate with a slice of lemon.

Beachcomber: put 4–6 cracked ice cubes into a cocktail shaker. Pour 150 ml/5 fl oz guava juice, 2 measures lime juice and 1 measure raspberry syrup over the ice. Shake vigorously until a frost forms, then pour into a chilled tumbler.

Melon Medley

Choose a very ripe, sweet-fleshed melon, such as a cantaloupe, for this lovely, fresh-tasting cocktail. This drink is perfect for sipping on a hot evening.

serves 1

4–6 crushed ice cubes
60 g/2 oz diced melon flesh
4 measures orange juice
½ measure lemon juice

❶ Put the crushed ice cubes into a blender and add the diced melon. Pour in the orange juice and lemon juice. Blend until slushy.

❷ Pour into a chilled Collins glass.

Sweet and juicy

River Cruise (to serve 6): put 450 g/1 lb diced cantaloupe melon flesh into a blender or food processor and process to a smooth purée. Scrape the purée into a jug. Put the peel and juice of 2 lemons and 2 tablespoons sugar into a small saucepan. Heat gently, stirring until the sugar has dissolved. Pour the lemon syrup over the melon purée and set aside to cool, then cover with clingfilm and chill in the refrigerator for at least 2 hours. To serve, half fill six chilled tumblers with cracked ice. Stir the melon mixture and divide it between the glasses. Top up with sparkling mineral water and decorate with melon wedges and cocktail cherries.

Kool Kevin: put 4–6 crushed ice cubes into a blender and add 60 g/2 oz diced cantaloupe melon flesh, 1 measure grenadine and 1 measure double cream. Blend until smooth then pour into a chilled tumbler. Add 1 measure ginger ale and stir gently. Sprinkle with ground ginger and decorate with a wedge of melon.

Glossary

Amaretto: almond-flavoured liqueur from Italy

Amer Picon: French apéritif bitters, flavoured with orange and gentian

Angostura bitters: rum-based bitters from Trinidad

Anisette: French liqueur, flavoured with anise, coriander and other herbs

Applejack: North American name for apple brandy (see Fruit Brandies)

Aquavit: Scandinavian grain spirit, usually flavoured with caraway

Armagnac: French brandy produced in Gascony – it is rarely used for cocktails

Bacardi: leading brand of white rum, originally from Cuba and now produced in Bermuda – also the name of a cocktail

Bailey's Irish Cream: Irish, whiskey-based, chocolate flavoured liqueur

Bénédictine: French, monastic liqueur flavoured with herbs, spices and honey

Bitters: a flavour-enhancer made from berries, roots and herbs

Bourbon: American whiskey made from a mash that must contain at least 51 per cent corn

Brandy: spirit distilled from fermented grapes, although many fruit brandies are based on other fruits (see Fruit brandy)

Calvados: French apple brandy from Normandy

Campari: Italian bitters flavoured with quinine

Champagne: French sparkling wine from La Champagne, produced under strictly controlled conditions

Chartreuse: French monastic liqueur flavoured with a secret recipe of herbs – green Chartreuse is stronger than yellow

Cobbler: long, mixed drink traditionally based on sherry but now made from spirits and other ingredients

Coconut liqueur: coconut-flavoured, spirit-based liqueur – Malibu is the best-known brand

Coffee liqueur: coffee-flavoured, spirit-based liqueur – Tia Maria, based on Jamaican rum, and Kahlúa from Mexico are the best-known brands

Cointreau: best-selling brand of triple sec (see Triple sec), flavoured with sweet Mediterranean oranges and Caribbean bitter orange peel

Collins: a spirit-based cocktail topped up with a carbonated soda, such as ginger ale

Crème de banane: banana-flavoured liqueur

Crème de cacao: French, chocolate-flavoured liqueur, produced in various strengths and colours

Crème de cassis: blackcurrant-flavoured liqueur, mainly from France

Crème de framboise: raspberry-flavoured liqueur

Crème de menthe: mint-flavoured liqueur – may be white or green

Crème de noyaux: liqueur made from apricot and peach kernels

Crème violette: violet-flavoured liqueur

Crème Yvette: American Parma violet-flavoured liqueur

Curaçao: orange-flavoured liqueur, produced mainly in France and the Netherlands, but originating from the Caribbean – available in a range of colours including white, orange and blue

Drambuie: Scotch whisky-based liqueur, flavoured with honey and heather

Dry gin: see Gin

Dubonnet: wine-based apéritif, flavoured with quinine – available red and blonde

Eau-de-vie: spirit distilled from fruit – tends to be used (wrongly) as interchangeable with fruit brandy

Falernum: Caribbean syrup flavoured with fruit and spices

Fernet Branca: Italian liqueur with a bitter flavour

Fizz: long, mixed drink, based on spirits and made fizzy with soda water

Flip: spirit based, creamy mixed drink made with egg

Fruit brandy: strictly speaking, brandy is distilled from fermented grapes, but many fruit brandies are distilled from whatever the fruit type is, such as apple and apricot – plum brandy, also known as slivovitz, is usually made from Mirabelle and Switzen plums

Galliano: Italian liqueur, flavoured with honey and vanilla

Genever: also known as Hollands and Dutch gin, the original gin, which is sweeter and fuller-flavoured than London, Plymouth or dry gin – rarely used in cocktails (see Gin)

Gin: a colourless, grain-based spirit, strongly flavoured with juniper and other herbs. London, Plymouth and dry gin are most commonly used for cocktails

Gomme Syrup: sweet syrup from France

Grand Marnier: French, orange flavoured, Cognac-based liqueur

Grappa: fiery, Italian spirit distilled from wine must

Grenadine: non-alcoholic, pomegranate-flavoured syrup –

used for sweetening and colouring cocktails

Irish whiskey: unblended spirit made from malted or unmalted barley and some other grains – suitable for many cocktails

Julep: originally a sweet syrup, now a family of spirit-based cocktails, flavoured and decorated with fresh mint

Kahlúa: popular Mexican brand of coffee liqueur

Kirsch: colourless cherry-flavoured eau-de-vie, mainly from France and Switzerland

Kümmel: colourless Dutch liqueur, flavoured with caraway

Lillet: French herb-flavoured liqueur, based on wine and Armagnac

Liqueur: distilled spirit flavoured with such things as fruit, herbs, coffee, nuts, mint and chocolate

London gin: the driest gin (see Gin)

Madeira: fortified wine from the island of the same name

Malibu: leading brand of coconut liqueur – based on rum

Mandarine Napoléon: Belgian, brandy-based liqueur flavoured with tangerines

Maraschino: Italian, cherry-flavoured liqueur – usually colourless, but may be red

Martini: popular Italian brand of vermouth produced by Martini and Rossi and also the name of a classic cocktail

Melon liqueur: spirit-based, melon-flavoured liqueur – Midori is the leading brand

Midori: Japanese liqueur (see Melon Liqueur)

Noilly Prat: leading French brand of very dry vermouth

Orgeat: almond-flavoured syrup

Pastis: aniseed-flavoured liqueur from France

Plymouth gin: a less dry type of gin than London gin (see Gin)

Port: Portuguese fortified wine that may be white, ruby or tawny – white and inexpensive ruby are most appropriate for cocktails

Pousse-Café: a drink poured in layers to float on top of one another, which gives its name to a narrow, straight-sided stemmed glass

Quinquina: French, wine-based apéritif, flavoured with quinine

Rickey: a spirit-based cocktail including lemon or lime juice and soda water

Rum: spirit distilled from fermented sugar cane juice or molasses – light, golden and dark have distinctive flavours and all are widely used, together and severally, in cocktails and punches

Rye whiskey: mainly American and Canadian whiskey which must be made from a mash containing at least 51 per cent rye

Sake: Japanese rice wine

Sambuca: Italian, liquorice-flavoured liqueur

Schnapps: grain-based spirit – available in a range of flavours, including peach and peppermint

Scotch whisky: blends are a mixture of about 40 per cent malt and 60 per cent grain whisky and are most suitable for cocktails – single malts should be drunk neat or diluted with water

Slammer: a cocktail mixed by slamming it on the bar

Slivovitz: plum brandy (see Fruit brandy)

Sloe gin: Liqueur made by steeping sloes in gin – previously homemade but now available commercially

Sour: a spirit-based cocktail containing sugar, and lemon or lime juice

Southern Comfort: American whiskey-based, peach-flavoured liqueur

Strega: Italian, herb-flavoured liqueur

Sugar syrup: a sweetener for cocktails, made by dissolving sugar in boiling water (see page 7)

Swedish Punsch: aromatic rum-based drink, flavoured with wines and syrups

Tequila: Mexican spirit distilled from pulque from fermented maguey cacti

Tia Maria: popular, Jamaican rum-based coffee liqueur

Triple sec: colourless, orange-flavoured liqueur

Vermouth: wine-based apéritif flavoured with extracts of wormwood – both sweet and dry vermouths are widely used in cocktails

Vodka: colourless, grain-based spirit, originally from Russia and Poland. Flavoured vodkas, such as lemon, raspberry and chilli, are becoming increasingly popular

Whisky: spirit distilled from grain or malted barley – the main types are bourbon, rye, Irish and Scotch

Cocktail List

- Acapulco *40* • American Rose *16* • Bloody Mary *54*

- Buck's Fizz *62* • Carolina *72* • Classic Cocktail *10*

- Crocodile *74* • Cuba Libre *44* • Daiquiri *42*

- Frozen Daiquiri *66* • Full Monty *78* • Grapefruit Cooler *88*

- Kir *60* • Lip Smacker *84* • Little Prince *86*

- Long Island Iced Tea *36* • Mai Tai *48* • Manhattan *22*

- Margarita *50* • Martini *26* • Melon Medley *92*

- Mint Julep *18* • Moscow Mule *56* • Old Fashioned *24*

- Piña Colada *38* • Screwdriver *58* • Salty Dog *28*

- Shirley Temple *90* • Sidecar *12* • Singapore Sling *34*

- Stinger *14* • Tequila Slammer *68* • Tequila Sunrise *52*

- Tom Collins *32* • Vodga *76* • What the Hell *80*

- Whiskey Sour *20* • White Lady *30* • Wild Night Out *70*

- Zombie *46*